ANGIE WARD

BEYOND CHURCH AND PARA CHURCH

FROM COMPETITION TO
MISSIONAL EXTENSION

FOREWORD BY Jerry E. White

ivp

An imprint of InterVarsity Press
Downers Grove, Illinois

Pro Ecclesia et Pro Regnum

(For the church and for the kingdom)

InterVarsity Press
P.O. Box 1400 | Downers Grove, IL 60515-1426
ivpress.com | email@ivpress.com

InterVarsity Press® is the publishing division of InterVarsity Christian Fellowship/USA®. For more information, visit intervarsity.org.

All Scripture quotations, unless otherwise indicated, are taken from The Holy Bible, New International Version®, NIV®. Copyright © 1973, 1978, 1984, 2011 by Biblica, Inc.™ Used by permission of Zondervan. All rights reserved worldwide. www.zondervan.com. The "NIV" and "New International Version" are trademarks registered in the United States Patent and Trademark Office by Biblica, Inc.™

While any stories in this book are true, some names and identifying information may have been changed to protect the privacy of individuals.

The publisher cannot verify the accuracy or functionality of website URLs used in this book beyond the date of publication.

Cover design: Faceout Studio, Tim Green
Interior design: Daniel van Loon
Image: © by Ruhey / Moment via Getty Images

ISBN 978-1-5140-0957-4 (print) | ISBN 978-1-5140-0958-1 (digital)

Printed in the United States of America ∞

Library of Congress Cataloging-in-Publication Data
A catalog record for this book is available from the Library of Congress.

31 30 29 28 27 26 25 | 12 11 10 9 8 7 6 5 4 3 2 1

"Do you feel like all we have is bad news about the church and stories of divisive hostile competition between Christians? How can we be the body of Christ, properly functioning together for the gospel advance in our generation? *Beyond Church and Parachurch* reveals the way forward."
Carmen LaBerge, radio host, kingdom communicator, and author

"Angie Ward has rightly recognized the need for a book-length study of parachurch ministry for the twenty-first century. While brief and accessible, *Beyond Church and Parachurch* gives attention to history, sociology, missiology, and most importantly, theology in helping readers understand the issues."
Mikey Lynch, editorial director for The Gospel Coalition Australia

"This volume is a worthy, timely, and provocative contribution to a vitally important topic that is widely misunderstood, particularly in the Protestant world. If applied today, these insights would greatly enhance our overall kingdom effectiveness and powerfully enhance our missional synergy."
Sam Metcalf, president emeritus of Novo-US

"Angie says the church must be missional in its role as a community, servant, and messenger in the world, while parachurches are missional extensions into one or other of those areas. That kind of thinking just might break the logjam in this discussion. Angie Ward's book is a winsome mix of solid ecclesiology, excellent missiology, and a deep love for God's people."
Michael Frost, founder of the Tinsley Institute at Morling College

"Drawing on robust ecclesiology that emphasizes the value and power of the local church, Dr. Ward shows how churches and parachurch organizations might come to think of themselves, and each other, as partners within the same missional ecosystem, opening up fresh ways of moving from competition to collaboration."
Ryan Tafilowski, chair of the Department of Theology at Denver Seminary

"Angie's book makes a compelling contribution to this urgent yet often overlooked conversation, adroitly integrating theology and history with examples and practical application. This is for every church, every nonprofit, and for every Christian who seeks to understand God's design for the church reaching the world."
Scott Harris, vice president of church and global engagement, Mission Increase

"Angie Ward calls us out of our ecclesial silos to reclaim a collaborative relationship between the church and parachurch organizations. In this timely and important book, Ward's practical recommendations for working together as one, unified body will be essential as the American church faces challenges in the post-institutional era."

Jayne Wilcox, assistant professor of theology at Ashland Theological Seminary

"Angie Ward has given us an important, bold, and constructively thought-provoking book. In an era of individual deconstruction and 'churchless' Christianity, she calls upon Christians—as individuals, churches, and organizations—to think, be, and do together in ways that will more effectively advance God's work in the world."

W. David Buschart, professor of theology and historical studies at Denver Seminary

"A groundbreaking guide for Christian leaders seeking to bridge gaps and break silos in ministry. Angie Ward draws from her deep expertise to challenge traditional paradigms and offer a compelling vision for integrated ministry. With thought-provoking case studies and practical strategies, this book is essential for anyone who desires to see the whole church working together for the sake of the whole world. This is not just a book— it's a call to action that will reshape your framework and approach to ministry, equipping you to serve with clarity and unity."

Meredith King, author of Immovable and founder of True to Life Ministries

"The one book you need to demystify the complicated history and future of the church and parachurch relationship."

Kelli J. Smith, vice president of church engagement at The MomCo

"Angie advocates for a redefined understanding of the church/parachurch relationship and suggests a new paradigm for these structures to both empower and release individual believers to express their God-given calling that the whole church might truly take the whole gospel to the whole world."

Matt Owens, regional director for East Asia at VisionSynergy

"This book will challenge and inspire you to reclaim your ecclesiology, reframe your perspective on ministry, and revolutionize your understanding of God's kingdom work. . . . Discover how God designed the body of Christ as a connected ecosystem and find your unique role within it. A must-read for ministry leaders seeking deeper kingdom impact!"

Heather Karls Chaniott, CEO of Missions Development International

CONTENTS

FOREWORD

In the forty years since I wrote *The Church and the Parachurch: An Uneasy Marriage*, little has changed, yet everything has changed. Tensions still exist between local churches and mission movements (parachurch agencies). Theology, competition, money, and perception still pervade the landscape of the church. But we have experienced seismic changes in our culture and technology, and in both local churches and mission agencies. Mainline denominations are shrinking. Megachurches continue to grow and break into smaller church bodies. New local congregations appear daily. In the mission agency world, we have an explosion of new ministries. The larger mission agencies still exist and grow, and have not disappeared as some predicted. Digital technology profoundly affects both local congregations and local and international agencies, opening more startups and diminishing church attendance.

Dr. Angie Ward's *Beyond Church and Parachurch* is a welcome and needed book addressing the current tensions and opportunities. Dr. Ward addresses history even before the Reformation in a concise and new way. She lays out our current tensions and conflicts with clarity and grace. She is a strong supporter of the primal place of the local congregation, yet theologically and practically stating the legitimacy and necessity of mission agencies both locally and internationally. She calls for a unifying of our imperative to proclaim the kingdom and the gospel to the ends of the earth.

In the eyes of the world, our disunity in the evangelical segment of the religious world terribly hurts our witness of Christ and his church. They see squabbling and an unfocused proclamation that both confuses and hinders the evangelical movement of the gospel. We can do better. And we must. The disunity comes from both church and agency sides. We all bear the responsibility for unity and love. We all passionately believe in the mission to proclaim the gospel of Jesus Christ to a needy and lost world.

Dr. Ward's foundational book points us to a way forward. I am enthused at what this book can do to lead us as church leaders and agency leaders to a new synergy. Yet a book does not make it happen. Leaders and lay men and women are the agents of change, guided by the Holy Spirt and the Scriptures. Let's impact the twenty-first century together for the cause of the kingdom.

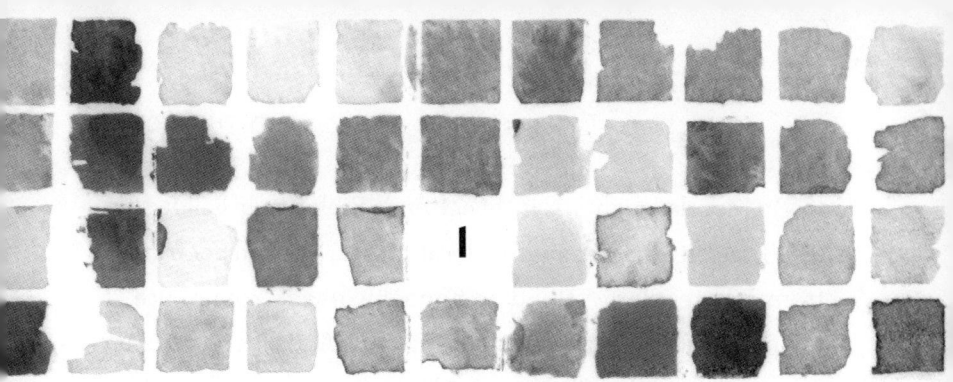

WHY THIS BOOK?

AN INTRODUCTION AND A ROAD MAP

Cynthia is a forty-two-year-old mother of three sons, ages eight to fifteen. Each week she attends Sunday-morning worship services at House of Hope church, a nondenominational congregation that was planted thirty years ago by a group of Christians who left a mainline denominational church when their longtime pastor moved out of state for an assignment to another congregation. Cynthia's boys attend Sunday school during one of the two morning service times, while her two teenagers return on Sunday evening for middle-school and high-school youth group.

Cynthia is a regular volunteer in the children's ministry at House of Hope. She also helps lead a kids' Bible study at her youngest son's elementary school. All three boys grew up going to Bible Club. The oldest son, now in high school, attends Fellowship of Christian Athletes on Thursday mornings. Every September, he and his middle-school brother spend one Wednesday morning praying for their classmates at See You at the Pole.

On Monday nights, Cynthia attends Bible Study Fellowship (BSF), which is held at another local church. She and her friends from BSF regularly attend an annual women's conference at the professional sports arena downtown. And whether on her way to Bible Club, BSF, House of Hope church, or to her job as an office manager for a landscaping company, Cynthia listens either to worship music on the local Christian radio station, or a podcast or an audiobook by a well-known Christian speaker or author.

Cynthia is a typical evangelical Protestant Christian in the United States today. You probably know a number of Cynthias, or people quite like her. Perhaps you *are* a Cynthia.

Or perhaps you are more like Lucas, the senior pastor at House of Hope church, now in his sixth year there and his fourteenth year in church ministry. Although House of Hope is not part of a denomination, it is a member of a national network of churches focused on reaching their communities with the good news of Jesus Christ. Lucas is also a member of a monthly coaching group provided by a different national network.

In addition to weekly worship gatherings and its regular in-house activities, House of Hope runs a teen ministry in a local trailer park as well as a thriving youth soccer ministry, including leagues and coaching, on its ten-acre property. These ministries are staffed primarily by volunteer college students from the nearby university, although most of these students don't attend House of Hope because they are involved with the student ministry organizations that meet on campus. Some of the full-time staff from these organizations, as well as from the local pregnancy center, attend House of Hope church. Lucas was recently asked to join the board of the pregnancy center, and the church gives some of its income to this ministry.

The House of Hope congregation also sponsors several overseas missionaries through a variety of agencies focusing on various parts of the world. Lucas receives repeated requests for House of Hope to support the college ministries and other organizations around town, which he has learned usually means a desire for regular financial contributions, promotion of their programs, and/or announcements about the volunteer needs in those ministries. Lucas, however, wishes House of Hope had enough volunteers for its *own* programs, including Sunday school and the nursery.

Then there's Jasmine, a twenty-something staff worker with ULife, one of the campus ministries at the university. Jasmine came to Christ through her organization's influence on her own college campus and has a passion for reaching students with the gospel. Jasmine attends a different church in town. She sometimes wishes she could be more involved in her church, but her work with college students means that evenings and weekends are often dedicated to activities on campus, including a weekly large-group worship gathering. Jasmine gives some of her limited income—which she must fundraise for herself as a campus "missionary"—to the church, and some to support her own campus ministry. Can you identify with her?

Welcome to the complex world of Christian life and ministry in the twenty-first century. Cynthia, Lucas, and Jasmine are amalgamations, but they are not anomalies. The snapshots of their lives give us a glimpse into a vast collection of churches and Christian organizations that are both connected to and competitive with one another.

Yes, I said *competitive with*. Those of us who work in Christian ministry may say or even believe we're all on the "same team," but the reality is that all of our organizations have their own agendas, and those agendas often contend for the same people and resources. In the day-to-day struggle for market share, or just for simple survival, precious little time is spent on considering how all of us—churches, Christian organizations, the pastors and leaders of these organizations, and the people in the pews—relate to one another, much less how they *should* relate. I believe this is because the people of God suffer from a fundamental deficit in ecclesiology—that is, a theological understanding of what the church is, what it should be, and what it should do.

Why does this matter? Lest you think that *ecclesiology* is just a ten-dollar word, a seminary term, or a purely academic concern, let me make this bold claim: Jesus' teaching, indeed all of the New Testament, makes the case that our ecclesiology— our understanding of "church"—is central to our very *identity*.

You see, as followers of Jesus Christ, the Scriptures clearly teach that we are not just individual believers—we are members of Christ's body, the church (1 Cor. 12:27). In other words, "church" is not just a building we visit, an event we attend, or a group of people we hang out with. It is *who we are*—a collective *identity*. Let me say it another way: you and I *are* the church, the body of Christ.

Read that again, slowly: You. and. I. *are*. the. church.

WE. ARE.

It doesn't get more central than that. Church, and our belonging in it, is a state of *being,* not just a behavior.

And yet we are more inclined to argue over the style of music in a worship gathering, the role of women in ministry, or the events of the end times than to spend time seeking to understand who we are and the significance of this identity for our lives both individually and corporately. Meanwhile, whether or not we are aware of it, this lack of understanding affects our work *and* our witness. How could it not? An understanding of our identity is critical to everything we as the body of Christ say and do in his name. It affects not only our ministry, but also our unity, and Jesus' prayerful plea for the church was that it would be marked by unity.

I think we can do better. I think we *must* do better.

We live in a world in desperate need for the good news of Jesus Christ. There are millions of people far from God and millions more who claim the name of Christ yet live nothing like Christ commanded his followers. Just five minutes scrolling through the day's headlines—or for that matter, five minutes spent driving around our communities—reminds us of the realities of mental illness, violence, abuse, poverty, disease, death, and broken relationships with God and with one another. Whether close to home or across the globe, the needs are evident and abundant, even overwhelming. Come, Lord Jesus.

Yet we also live in a world, particularly a Western world, where there are more churches and Christian ministries than ever before in history. More efforts than ever, yet statistics and our own experience tell us that much of the world is moving farther from God, not closer.

Even Christians are becoming less "Christian" in terms of both beliefs and behaviors. Evangelicalism is increasingly fracturing. By any measure, the primacy of the Western church is in decline. Individual Christians of all ages are deconstructing their faith and rethinking the nature, purpose, and necessity of the church. Many people stopped attending church during the pandemic and didn't come back. Christians are disillusioned with abusive church leaders and have given up on organized church. Christian higher education is facing demographic shrinkage, as fewer kids in youth group means fewer students in Christian colleges and seminaries.

As a result, a greater number of organizations are competing for a continuously shrinking pool of human, financial, and material resources. The urgency of unmet needs combined with a scarcity of resources leads to a nagging sense of anxiety that can make pastors and ministry leaders feel defensive and territorial.

It would be easy to blame all sorts of outside factors for this continued decline: secularization, the wrong political leaders, the culture, the media, the entertainment industry— pick your enemy. Yet I think that blame is misguided. You see, after nearly a decade of reading, researching, thinking, serving in, observing, teaching, and talking about this thing called "church," I am fully convinced that our problem is that the church—and by that I mean the global collection of believers who the Bible says comprises the body of Christ, but in particular the Western, and more specifically, the United

States church—does not have a clear sense of what it, what *we*, should be and do.

In other words, I believe the calls are coming from inside the house.

More than fifteen years ago, Darrell Guder presciently wrote, "The answer to the crisis of the North American church will not be found at the level of method and problem solving. . . . It has to do with who we are and what we are for."[1] Today, the need for redefinition is more urgent than ever.

When I bring this up with other men and women serving in churches and Christian ministries, I am met with wholehearted affirmation, often accompanied by frustration or sadness. No matter their affiliation or role—church or Christian organization, leader or lay volunteer—there is a sense that something isn't working, that we need clarity, that the whole does not currently equal the sum of its parts, that it could and should be better.

Our lack of clarity and unity leads us to what I described at the start of this chapter. We spend a lot of time, energy, and money—most of it for wonderful causes, and for some progress, sure; but still, overall we operate in and from our own silos. At best, we are wasting or duplicating our efforts. At worst, we are actually laboring at cross purposes. But what if the church had a clear understanding of its identity and its mission and the whole church worked together for the whole world?

CHURCH AND PARACHURCH

Much of this conversation has historically been framed in terms of the relationship between two entities: the church and what is often known as the "parachurch." We'll talk about that term a lot more throughout this book, but for now suffice to say that the parachurch generally refers to the constellation of dozens of types of Christian organizations, including the ULife ministry that Jasmine works for, the pregnancy center on whose board Lucas sits, and the Fellowship of Christian Athletes chapter that Cynthia's son attends. The true-to-life descriptions of Cynthia, Lucas, and Jasmine demonstrate how intertwined these entities are. But you likely already know this from your own experience, as I do.

I was literally born into the church, or at least into a church-related entity: a Catholic hospital in Milwaukee, Wisconsin. A few days later I was picked up by representatives from Catholic Social Services, to whom my biological mother had turned when she decided to give me up for adoption. I was placed into a Catholic adoptive family and baptized into the Roman Catholic Church as an infant. When I was old enough, I began attending CCD, the Catholic Church's religious education program for children.

My parents left the Catholic Church just before my First Communion (age eight) to attend a Protestant evangelical church. This was the late 1970s, and my mom went all-in on that church and the attendant evangelical subculture of the next several decades. Our house was filled with the voices of Chuck Swindoll and Charles Stanley on the Christian radio station; the television featured Jimmy Swaggart and *The 700 Club*. Our tables displayed the latest books by Christian authors such as James Dobson and Tim LaHaye. Every Wednesday, for decades, my mother hosted a Friendship Bible Coffee group at our house. Just before I entered sixth grade, my parents decided I would start attending a Christian school. In middle school, I also got more involved in our church youth ministry, but I didn't stop there. I went to church youth group *and* Campus Life. I attended winter retreats at area Christian camps.

After high school, I attended a Christian college where a bunch of us would carpool nearly an hour every Sunday to attend an up-and-coming church called Willow Creek. I majored in youth ministry and went to work at a year-round Christian camp right after graduating. I then moved to Denver for seminary where I met and married a guy who had been very involved with InterVarsity Christian Fellowship during his college years. Over the next twenty-five years, his pastoral ministry took us to five churches in three states. Meanwhile, I worked in church and parachurch youth ministry and eventually earned my doctorate from another seminary. I then taught at several Christian colleges and seminaries where my students were involved with every type of church, camp, denomination, educational institution, evangelistic organization, student ministry, missionary agency, and social service organization imaginable.

I now work at Denver Seminary as the director of our Doctor of Ministry program, continuing to encourage and equip women and men for all types of ministry around the world. I've even published a few books with Christian publishers. In other words, I have impeccable Christian credentials. (Please notice my tongue planted firmly in cheek.)

It's true, though, that I've been immersed in the world of the church and in Christian ministry for decades. Within it, I've seen and experienced almost everything you could imagine. Yet, quite miraculously, I'm still in love with the church. And it's because I love the church that I believe this book is essential for our day and age.

FOR THE TWENTY-FIRST CENTURY

In 1983, Dr. Jerry White, at the time a staff member with The Navigators, wrote a book titled *The Church and the Parachurch: An Uneasy Marriage.* In it, he described the tensions he observed between the world of the church and the world of the parachurch along with recommendations for resolving the problems and issues he saw. White would go on to become president of The Navigators, serving for nearly twenty years before retiring into the active position of International President Emeritus.

The Church and the Parachurch was part of a series of "Critical Concerns" books, indicating the topic's perceived importance when it was published. And while people who have read White's book over the years have raved about it and articulated the need for an updated follow-up volume, no one picked up the baton for forty years.[2] Yet during that time, the concerns first raised by White have become even more critical, as the church and culture have dramatically shifted and evolved.

I first read *The Church and the Parachurch* when I was preparing for a new course I had designed for my doctoral students, "Reclaiming Ecclesiology: Faithful Foundations for Effective Ministry." My boss at the time wasn't sure the course would attract enough students to be able to make it go. To the surprise of both of us, the course drew the largest enrollment of the semester and has become one of our most popular electives. Some of my students were so impacted that they changed the course of their doctoral research or even the focus and methods of their ministry. This just underscored to me the tremendous need for teaching and conversation on this topic.

After my first time teaching this course, I was able to meet Jerry White in person and thank him for his seminal book and his ongoing work. That conversation led to additional conversations and connections, which then led to Jerry and I working with several others to convene a Church and Parachurch Leaders' Summit in Denver. More than thirty leaders from around the country, their ministries spanning the globe, convened to foster understanding and further the conversation. Once again, it became clear that we had touched a nerve and tapped into a need.

At Jerry's encouragement and with his blessing, I am committed to continuing what he started. Although church and parachurch organizations impact every believer, every leader, and every location around the globe, few up-to-date resources comprehensively examine the nature of and relationship between these entities, and their significance for the kingdom of God, the local church, and the individual believer.

Our missional moment demands that we engage this conversation more urgently. Yet we must do so from a posture of humility and a desire for cooperation for the good of the kingdom. The next generation of Christians and ministry leaders must chart a path for the future of the church for the world. It is to those ends that I have written this book, and I invite you to embark on this endeavor with me.

WHERE WE'RE GOING

Each chapter in this book is organized around a guiding question. Over the course of ten chapters, we will look at the current state of the church in its various forms, explore the history and theology of church and parachurch, and examine models, relationships, and challenges. Once we've done that, I will set forth a comprehensive new way of thinking for the church for the twenty-first century and beyond. This suggested paradigm recognizes and incorporates multiple organizational expressions while challenging leaders of these expressions, as well as everyday Christians, to both theological faithfulness and generous partnership in order to meet the world's greatest needs.

This book combines my passion for the church with my training and bent as a scholar and teacher. I approached this project from my own curiosity and the desire to be an open-minded learner, and I encourage you to do the same. Other authors have written about these issues as apologists within a particular organizational context—usually missionary agencies or local churches—or from a singular external perspective, whether historical, organizational, sociological, or theological. Here I have attempted to describe the overall landscape and integrate all of these perspectives into a comprehensive new framework. Although I have a lifetime of ministry experience, I learned a lot as I researched and wrote this book. I hope you make new discoveries and connections as well.

Whether you are a pastor or church leader, a staff member at a parachurch organization, a lay volunteer, or a member of the body of Christ who faithfully fills the pew each Sunday, I hope that this book will be provocative, but not toward conflict. Rather, I pray that it will provoke reflection and conversation, a deeper love for and sense of connection to the church in all its various expressions, and ultimately, changes in the way we "are" and "do" church.

Imagine a world in which Cynthia, Lucas, and Jasmine—along with the leaders and partakers of the Christian radio station, the children's ministry, Bible Club, FCA, See You at the Pole, BSF, youth group, the trailer park teen ministry, the soccer ministry, ULife and other college campus ministries, the missionary agencies, the pregnancy center, and *you* and *your* ministry—all saw themselves as part of a larger, interconnected ecosystem.

And what if this ecosystem was not just a theory or a purely cognitive framework, but the foundational paradigm that drove everyday practice for *every* member of the body of Christ? Think of how it might change how we view other parts of the body, from individuals to organizations. Think of how it might force us to change our own programs, participation, and postures. And think of the lives changed: not just those impacted by these ministries as they forged meaningful partnerships, but especially our own as we truly embraced our identity and calling as the church!

2

WHERE ARE WE?

THE STATE OF THE CHURCH, THE PARACHURCH, AND A WORLD IN NEED

The first responsibility of a leader is to define reality.

MAX DEPREE

Much is being written about the state of the church today. Some of it is hopeful, while many reports from the field describe gloom and doom scenarios. But what is reality, both in the Western world and around the globe?

As we begin our dive into the church-parachurch conversation, we need to first survey the landscape to gain an accurate picture of our current realities pertaining to the local church, parachurch organizations, charitable giving, and the needs around the world.

THE GREAT RUMMAGE SALE

When I lived in the midwestern United States, rummage sales—also called garage sales or yard sales—were a big thing every spring and summer. As soon as the weather got warm, signs would appear at the entrances to subdivisions and around neighborhoods announcing the addresses of the sales that weekend. If you drove past any of those homes, you'd see all manner of furniture, clothing, appliances, lawn and garden equipment, and other household items spread over tables set up in the front yard or in driveways. Some sales were well-organized while others looked quite chaotic. Either way, it was the season for cleaning out the basement and the attic, for shedding unwanted stuff, for getting rid of the old to make room for the new.

"About every five hundred years," the late Anglican Bishop Mark Dyer noted, "the Church feels compelled to hold a giant rummage sale."[1] In other words, at approximately five-hundred-year intervals the church undergoes a great house cleaning: rearranging, throwing out, or even overthrowing existing structures and institutions to bring renewal and new growth.[2]

The first such rummage sale in Christian history began in the late sixth century under Pope Gregory I, also known as Gregory the Great, who consolidated the church's power and led the re-forming and revitalization of society after the fall of the Roman Empire. The second was the Great Schism between the Eastern Christian churches and the Western (Roman) church in 1054. And the rummage sale we are most familiar with is the Great Reformation, which officially began when Martin Luther nailed his ninety-five theses to a door in Wittenberg, Germany, in 1517.

Every five hundred years . . . a giant rummage sale . . . and the last one was in the 1500s . . .

Count five hundred years forward from 1517 and we are . . . *here*.

While the rummage sale theory is not absolutely predictive—the Holy Spirit is not bound by a human timetable—history still tends to run in observable cycles. And by all signs, we are in the midst of another such upheaval. Almost anywhere you live, you can see the signs of a massive, global, church-wide rummage sale. The particular signs and effects may vary depending on your vantage point, but all reports indicate a seismic shift from the way things have been for the last several hundred years. And as with any major upheaval, no one knows exactly where things will land. Let's drive around a bit and spend some time walking among the tables to get a sense of the trends and shifts taking place in contemporary Christianity.

THE STATE OF THE CHURCH

We'll start with the church in the United States, which is unquestionably undergoing a major reconfiguration. The changes have been so rapid that the latest reports are obsolete almost as soon as they have been published, but the overall trends are clear and striking.

In 1945, 75 percent of American adults were members of a church, a number that held reasonably steady until 2000 (70 percent). Just twenty years later, that number had dipped to *47 percent*. The steepest declines can be seen among Gen-Xers and millennials: among the latter group (born 1981 to 1996), only 36 percent claimed formal membership in a church in 2020.[3]

In addition, while the initial declines were most drastic among mainline denominations and Christians who identified as progressive or liberal, more conservative branches of Christianity are no longer immune to the trends. The Southern Baptist Convention, the largest Protestant denomination in the United States, lost nearly half a million members in 2022 alone. Overall, SBC membership has experienced steady decline, from a peak of 16.3 million in 2006 to 13.2 million in 2022.[4]

The general decline in participation in church life can be seen on the ground in contracting congregations: the median congregation today has around 65 attendees, down from a median of 137 people in 2000.[5] As smaller congregations struggle to stay afloat, church closures have risen. In 2019, there were more church closures than openings in the United States,[6] and that was before the COVID-19 pandemic, which only exposed and accelerated the trends.

The decline in religious participation, which has been referred to as "the great dechurching," has been accompanied by a sharp increase in Americans who claim no religious affiliation (a.k.a. the "nones"), who now comprise about 28 percent of US adults.[7] While the latest data suggests that rise of the nones may be slowing overall, young adults continue to leave the church in droves.

In addition, trust in institutions and clergy continues to fall, as a host of highly public scandals and the #ChurchToo movement have rocked the religious landscape and organizations across the theological spectrum, from Roman Catholic to Southern Baptist to nondenominational churches and networks, leading to an unprecedented lack of public trust in the church, organized religion, and in individual clergy. As of 2024, fewer than one-third of Americans rated clergy as highly honest and ethical—lower than nurses, police officers, and chiropractors, although still higher than politicians, lawyers, and journalists.[8]

All this points to the largest and fastest religious shift in the history of the United States. "This is not a gradual shift," notes Jim Davis in his book *The Great Dechurching*. "It is a jolting one."[9] And this shift reflects similar trends throughout the Western world, including the UK, Canada, and Australia.[10] Meanwhile, the majority of the most secular countries in the world are located in Europe and Scandinavia.

Yet there are signs of hope on the margins. It must be noted that in the United States, almost all the decline of Christianity has been among *white* Americans. But in some denominations, such as the Roman Catholic Church, losses of white attendees have been offset by Hispanic immigration.[11] Elsewhere around the world, an unprecedented wave of displaced persons has taken a vibrant Christianity back to the Western countries that once sent missionaries to *them*. Simply put, immigrants and refugees are bringing with them a strong faith and building strong faith communities, reflecting a shift in influence in American society that can also be seen in the church worldwide. Even in the most secular countries in the Western world, there is a fresh hunger for the gospel of Jesus Christ as the good news is "new news" to those who grew up in non-Christian and post-Christian contexts, and who have found that science and reason have not answered the larger questions of life.[12]

It is well documented that the center of world Christianity has shifted from the West (Europe and North America) to the Global South, including Latin America, Asia, and Africa. Although the Christian conversion rate has not quite kept pace with global population growth, approximately one-third of the world's population professes Christian faith, and this number is predicted to rise steadily. In particular, Christianity has experienced explosive growth in China, it has doubled in Africa in just two decades, and 90 percent of Latin Americans claim involvement in a church, with many Christians switching from Catholicism to Pentecostalism, particularly in South America.[13]

THE STATE OF THE PARACHURCH

While the Western church in general and the American church in particular are experiencing significant decline, what has become commonly known as the parachurch sector has continued to grow. It is difficult to gain an accurate count of these types of organizations because of reporting requirements and classifications, but sociologist Christopher Scheitle calculated an informed estimate of around 20,000 religious public charities in the United States in 1997, which grew to 58,000 organizations just ten years later.[14] Today, according to some estimates there are over 100,000 distinct parachurch organizations in the United States alone and another 35,000 in the United Kingdom.[15]

In their book *The Prospering Parachurch*, Wesley Willmer, J. David Schmidt, and Martyn Smith developed a parachurch taxonomy, describing sixteen classifications of organizations that encompassed 208 unique types of organizations! Their broad categories included:

- Arts/Culture
- Associations
- Audiovisual/Media
- Camps/Conferences
- Constituency-Based Ministries
- Consulting
- Counseling/Guidance
- Education
- Environmental/Agricultural
- Evangelism
- Health Care
- Legal Assistance/Political Action
- Missions
- Printed Media
- Relief and Development
- Social Services[16]

Sociologist Christopher Scheitle later distilled these categories into ten primary sectors, from largest to smallest in terms of percentage of overall parachurch market share:

1. Charismatic Evangelism
2. Relief & Development
3. Education & Training
4. Publishing & Resources
5. Radio & Television
6. Missions & Missionary
7. Fellowship & Enrichment

8. Advocacy & Activism

9. Fund-Raising, Grant-Making & Other

10. Unspecific[17]

These categories encompass everything from televange-lists to K–12 Christian schools, to global missions agencies to justice ministries and charitable foundations, plus newer types of ministries that defy easy categorization, such as social media ministries and podcasts.

It's easy to see how these specialized organizations have enormous impact. No part of the world is untouched by their collective work. In fact, in some parts of the world, the para-church has saturated the religious landscape and everyday Christian experience.

But there's the rub: to many, the proliferation of parachurch organizations and their extended reach has come at the ex-pense of the authority, impact, and financial well-being of the local church. On the other hand, it could be argued from a social science perspective that churches and parachurch or-ganizations are part of an ever-changing religious market in which the decline of one entity—congregation, denomination, sector—is often accompanied by the rise of another. Is the parachurch the nemesis of the local congregation or simply a reimagining and reorganizing of the body of Christ within the broader religious landscape? At the very least, the parachurch is a force to be reckoned with.

THE STATE OF CHARITABLE GIVING

Speaking of financial well-being, let's look at trends in chari-table giving. The impact of such giving is irrefutable. Check out these statistics given by Peter Greer and Chris Horst in *Rooting for Rivals*:

- In American cities, the average church contributes approximately $150,000 of social services to their communities annually.

- Forty percent of the top fifty American charities are faith-based.

- Eighty percent of national hurricane and disaster recovery happens because of nonprofits, and 75 percent of those are faith-based.

- Faith-based organizations provide 30 to 70 percent of health care services in many African nations today.

- The work of faith-based organizations contributes to better health, lower infant mortality, lower corruption, greater literacy, higher educational attainment, and improved rights for women around the world.[18]

Giving makes a difference. But how is giving going these days?

After several years of record increases to help meet needs during the COVID-19 pandemic, charitable giving by individuals has declined slightly. The United States leads the world in charitable giving, voluntarily donating about seven times as much as continental Europeans and twice as much as Canadians.[19] However, while American households give an average of nearly 2 percent of their income to charitable causes, fewer of those dollars are going to churches. In the early 1980s, churches received over half of all charitable giving; today that proportion has dropped to less than one-third.[20]

This decline can be attributed to several factors. One is the overall decline in trust in churches. According to a recent Barna study, only 38 percent of Christians "completely trust" Christian churches with their financial support.[21] Another is that the number of older "loyalty" donors is declining. Young adults are less likely to attend church in the first place, and those who do have fewer resources to give.

But this doesn't mean that young adults aren't generous; they just give differently. "Next-gen" donors (Generation Z and millennials) prefer to support particular causes and issues, finding and supporting the one organization that they feel best represents their chosen cause. In addition, these donors are three times as likely to advocate for a particular organization compared to their parents and grandparents. For them, giving is only one part of their engagement with a cause. Younger adults want to be involved as volunteers and want charitable dollars to go more directly to social services. My personal experience bears this out, as I've talked with a number of young adults who don't believe churches will steward their money toward the greatest needs in their community or around the world. "Why should I give my money to pay for a fancy building or for more staff?" they ask.

These are important characteristics that will affect charitable giving for decades to come, as traditional donors (Gen X and Baby Boomers) pass their wealth on to next-gen donors:

> By some estimates, the greatest generational wealth transfer in the history of the world is already underway. Through 2045, some $84 trillion dollars will pass mostly

from baby boomers to Gen X and millennials. What's more, an estimated $12 trillion of that will find its way into philanthropy, either through foundations, donor-advised funds, impact investing, or personal direct action.[22]

THE STATE OF A WORLD IN NEED

The world's population currently stands at more than eight billion human beings. As the global population increases, the needs around the world also continue to multiply. Let's look at some of the most significant needs and crises across the globe and close to home.

Global displacement. The global population includes more than 115 million people who have been forcibly displaced worldwide as a result of persecution, conflict, violence, drought or floods, or human rights violations[23]—the largest number in history, with millions being added to the total every year. This global movement has created the largest wave of refugees to Europe since the end of World War II and has significantly changed the demographics of some cities and countries almost overnight. In addition, the epic number of displaced persons has created humanitarian crises around the world, as governments and other agencies are overwhelmed by unprecedented needs.

Poverty. Nearly one-quarter of the world's population—almost two billion people—live in impoverished conditions and dire circumstances. Children and youth make up two-thirds of the world's poor, and women are a majority in most impoverished regions. And while extreme poverty is largely concentrated to sub-Saharan Africa, poverty knows no boundaries: 19 percent of the world's poor live in developing countries, and more than eleven million children live in poverty in the United States, the richest country in the world.[24]

Evangelism. The global population of over eight billion consists of more than 17,000 people groups of which over 7,000 are classified as unreached people groups (UPGs), meaning that less than 2 percent of their population are evangelical Christians. Numbering almost 3.5 billion people, UPGs make up nearly 42 percent of the world's population, and 60 percent of them live in countries that are closed to missionaries from North America. Another 9.9 percent of the world's population—around 800 million people—are considered unevangelized peoples.[25]

Mental health. While many developed countries are considered "reached" from an evangelism perspective, these societies are now experiencing epidemic levels of depression and loneliness. The COVID-19 pandemic and its aftermath significantly affected the mental health of both adults and children in the United States and elsewhere, with impact disproportionately felt among the typically marginalized in society: racial and ethnic minority groups, mothers, children, those living in unstable housing situations, and people with disabilities or pre-existing mental illness. At the same time, substance abuse is on the rise, including alcohol abuse, opioid addiction, and prescription drug abuse.

IMPACT

What does all of this mean? We are clearly living in a time of major redistribution, a transitional period, a liminal space with no clear idea of where everything—including perhaps our own organizations, even ourselves—will land. In the words of David Bosch, "We live in a period of transition, on the borderline between a paradigm that no longer satisfies and one that is, to a large extent, still amorphous and opaque."[26]

When I lived in the midwestern United States, I could find a rummage sale every weekend. Where I live now in Colorado, snow skiing is a big thing and a "yard sale" takes on a completely different meaning. In ski country, a yard sale occurs when a skier or snowboarder crashes so hard that they lose their gear, scattering it across the slope as if they were hosting . . . well, a yard sale. While I am now officially retired from recreational skiing, I have had my share of yard sales over the years—and let me tell you, it is not a fun experience.

In a moment's time you lose the edge of your skis or your board, and suddenly you are flying through the air or rolling down a very cold and icy hill, completely out of control and anticipating a very uncomfortable landing. When you finally tumble to a stop, you first assess the condition of each of your various body parts, then attempt to ascertain the location of each piece of gear that was forcibly separated from you during your tumultuous episode.

To many of us, the current church-wide rummage sale is bringing similar feelings of disorientation, loss of control, and perhaps pain. The needs around us are ever greater, while the occupations, organizations, and frameworks that have oriented our lives may be undergoing significant changes, perhaps decline, even death or closure. Paradigm shifts, especially one like we are currently experiencing, are a radically disruptive and disequilibrating experience.

But as Bosch points out, "A time of paradigm change is, by nature, a time of crisis—and crisis, we remind ourselves, is the point where danger and opportunity meet."[27] In other words, the current reordering is also ripe with opportunities. At this missional moment, the need for the gospel is greater than it has ever been.

In exploring the rummage sale phenomenon in her book *The Great Emergence,* Phyllis Tickle points out three historically consistent results of such an upheaval:

1. A new and more vital form of Christianity emerges.

2. The dominant organized expression of Christianity at that time is "reconstituted" into a more pure, less hardened version of its former self.

3. "Every time the incrustations of an overly established Christianity have been broken open, the faith has spread—and been spread—dramatically into new geographic and demographic areas, thereby increasing exponentially the range and depth of Christianity's reach as a result of its time of unease and distress."[28]

Friends, we are living in an historic time, and we—*you and I,* as members of the body of Christ—have the opportunity to help reshape current encrustations of the church and the Christian faith into something more vital, more potent, and able to spread *dramatically* to every corner of the world. I can't think of anything more challenging, more dangerous, or more energizing.

3

HOW DID THIS ALL START?

CHURCH AND PARACHURCH IN THE
APOSTOLIC/CATHOLIC TRADITION

The morning bell roused Justin out of a deep slumber. He rubbed his eyes and squinted toward the small window in his room. It was still dark out, yet it was time to wake up. Within ten minutes, Justin had joined his fellow in-residence ministry workers for morning prayer in the chapel before their workday began—a day that would be punctuated by additional prayer gatherings before the noon meal and before an early bedtime. The rest of the day, Justin and his colleagues went about the work of God from their ministry center located on the edge of town.

The center was committed to serving the townspeople, many of whom were low-income folk. The center's programs and services included a school for children, a clinic for the sick and infirm, a guest house, and classes in farming and animal husbandry. Meanwhile, some full-time staff spent their days outside the center, cultivating the nearby farmland, selling products in the town, and feeding the poor in the community. All of these charitable efforts were supported by local believers, women and men who served as volunteers and donated material resources.

The type of work conducted by Justin and his co-workers in the name of Jesus Christ is nothing new. In fact, the center described here is not a contemporary nonprofit, but an eighth-century Benedictine monastery!

For millennia, the Great Commission (Mt 28:19-20) along with Jesus' command to "love your neighbor as yourself" (Mk 12:31) have motivated Christians to share the love and good news of Jesus Christ with their neighbors next door and those in need around the world. Over the course of church history these efforts have taken multiple forms through a variety of structures: some formal and officially sanctioned, others decidedly more organic or even underground.

While the term "parachurch" is relatively new, the concept has been around for a *long* time: not just since the twentieth century, the 1850s, or even the Second Great Awakening in the late 1700s, but for as long as the church has been in existence. The following chapters will trace the history of what is now frequently called the parachurch in the firm belief that understanding our history is critical to understanding the roots of tensions and the routes to greater partnership. As you read ahead, I encourage you to keep your own experiences and affiliations in mind, tracing them back through history for a greater appreciation for where and what they are today.

THE APOSTOLIC AGE

After Jesus' resurrection, his followers immediately went to work to fulfill his commands. The apostles Peter and John took the early lead, preaching boldly and performing acts of healing under the power of the Holy Spirit. Inspired by their example and similarly empowered by the Spirit, Acts 4 tells us that the early believers were marked by unity and radical generosity, sharing everything they had with the apostles, who then distributed it to those in need—a so-called "community of goods."[1] Indeed, Luke notes in Acts 4:33-35 that the early church was marked by both bold proclamation of the resurrection *and* the provision for material needs within the body of believers.

Just two chapters later, the apostles realized that they could not effectively carry out both of these efforts on their own. In response to complaints from Hellenistic Jews in the fellowship, the Twelve oversaw the selection of seven men to manage the daily distribution of food to widows and others in need so that they could focus on preaching (Acts 6:1-7). The fledgling church was already beginning to develop systems and structures for both broad evangelistic efforts and ministry to local needs.

The stoning of Stephen, who was one of the original overseers of the food distribution program, inaugurated a great persecution that led to the scattering of believers beyond Jerusalem. The scattered continued to spread the gospel to Jews and Gentiles, and a "great number of people believed and turned to the Lord" (Acts 11:21).

At this time, the church in Jerusalem still served as headquarters for the new community of believers. When the elders there heard about the effective evangelism of the Greeks in Antioch, they sent Barnabas to the city to assist with the numerical and spiritual growth of the church there. Barnabas soon brought Saul over to Antioch to join him, and the two spent a year ministering to the new fellowship. This ministry now included encouraging and teaching the local church and preaching to unbelievers (Acts 11:22-26). In addition, after several prophets from Jerusalem predicted a severe famine across the entire Roman world, the believers in Antioch collected gifts for Paul and Barnabas to send back to the elders for distribution to their Judean brothers and sisters (Acts 11:29-30).

While Peter continued to preach in Jerusalem, Barnabas and Saul worked from their home base of Antioch. But as more prophets and teachers were raised up there, the Holy Spirit instructed the church at Antioch to set apart Barnabas and Saul for a new work. The Antioch fellowship therefore became a "sending church" for the apostles' missionary endeavors—and indeed, the community at Antioch quickly became a missionary center for Syria and Asia Minor.[2]

Saul—by now known as Paul—took the gospel as far as Rome. Meanwhile, the original apostles continued to spread the good news of Jesus Christ around the known world: Peter traveled to Samaria, Joppa, Caesarea, and elsewhere from his home base in Jerusalem. John founded churches at Smyrna, Pergamos, Sardis, Philadelphia, Laodicea, and Thyatira. James "the Greater" (meaning older or taller), the brother of John, took the gospel to Spain, while James "the Lesser" ministered to the Jewish believers scattered abroad. Andrew preached around Asia. Mark, one of the "four evangelists" along with Matthew, Luke, and John, traveled with Paul and Barnabas and founded the church of Alexandria in Egypt. Matthew focused his ministry on Parthia and Ethiopia. Philip and Bartholomew preached in Greece, Phrygia, and Syria, while Thomas reached India.[3]

While the apostles maintained their itinerant ministry, the church at Jerusalem, and then at Antioch, became the seat of the expanding global church, meeting and ruling on matters of doctrine and church practice. The Council of Jerusalem (ca. AD 49) consisting of "the apostles and elders" determined that Gentile converts to Christianity did not need to be circumcised or maintain other Jewish rituals (Acts 15:1-35). However, Antioch's growing size, influence, and role as the base of Paul's missionary endeavors, followed by the fall of Jerusalem in AD 70, cemented the importance of the church at Antioch in the first centuries after Christ's death.

Even as overall authority centralized in Jerusalem and then Antioch, local churches busied themselves following the apostles' teaching. They gathered regularly for "communal eating and drinking, music, symbol, prayer, Scripture, [and] teaching"—what we today might call corporate worship. However, worship in the New Testament referred more to an ethos or a Christian way of life than to communal activities.[4] New Testament writers instructed Jesus' followers to practice more than thirty "one anothers," some focused on character and relationships and others on practices such as hospitality and bearing one another's burdens.

Early roles and responsibilities. The Bible refers to four roles in the earliest days of the church: apostle, prophet, elder, and disciple. The apostles referred to "the Twelve"—Jesus' original twelve disciples, with Matthias substituting for Judas Iscariot—plus Paul and Barnabas, who traveled beyond Jerusalem and Antioch, preaching the gospel and establishing and encouraging local churches. Prophets, including Agabus,

Judas Barsabbas, Silas, and the four unmarried daughters of Philip the evangelist (Acts 21:9), spoke God's truth to believers. Elders were a group of individuals appointed to oversee a particular gathering, and sometimes came together with the apostles to consider issues and decisions facing the church at large, as with the Council of Jerusalem. Disciples referred to the members of a local fellowship, that is, everyday Christians. With one another and under the oversight of the elders, they practiced their faith within their families, fellowships, and local communities.

The seven men chosen in Acts 6 to care for the daily needs of the Christian community were not formally named or titled. But by the time Paul wrote his letters to Timothy and Titus in the AD mid-sixties, a new role had been added: that of deacon. While Scripture only describes their qualifications and not their functions, the early church authorized deacons to take care of the physical and logistical needs of the church in keeping with the pattern found in Acts 6:1-6. From early on, then, "the apostolic age knew both a traveling group of Spirit-empowered leaders and a resident group caring for the needs of established congregations."[5]

The functional framework of apostles, presbyters/bishops/elders, and deacons of the early church mirrored the Jewish structure of prophets, priests, and Levites that prevailed until the destruction of Jerusalem and the fall of the Second Temple.[6] It continued to be utilized by the swiftly growing Gentile church and is commonly utilized, although frequently (especially in Protestantism) without a clear understanding of the role of the apostle or prophet, in a majority of the church today.

HOW DID THIS ALL START?

Authority structures. It is interesting to note that when Paul and Barnabas started a church, they would appoint its elders (Acts 14:23). In other words, the missionaries, serving as church planters, appointed the church leaders. The church leaders did not appoint and send the missionaries. The apostles' movement in these "missionary bands" was largely guided by the Holy Spirit, not by the decision of any church or group of churches. In today's missionary parlance, they were "field governed." For example, in Acts 16 Paul had planned to go to Asia but was "kept by the Holy Spirit from preaching the word" in that province. Instead, Paul had an overnight vision of a "man of Macedonia" asking Paul to come there and help them, which Paul did "at once" (Acts 16:6-10). There is no evidence that Paul discussed this change with the powers-that-were in Antioch. In addition, when Paul returned to Antioch between journeys, *he* would gather the church together to share what God had done during his travels. Again, there is no evidence that Paul, Barnabas, and others were asked or required to "report back" to the leaders there.[7]

At the same time, no one person or group was considered "parachurch" in the sense of being "alongside" the church. Everyone—apostles, prophets, elders, deacons, and disciples— was part of the church. Elders, deacons, and disciples were home-based while apostles and prophets were itinerant ministers, sometimes settling within a community for a period of time, as when Paul lived with Priscilla and Aquila in Corinth (Acts 18:1-4).

THE EARLY CHURCH

As the early church developed beyond the Apostolic Age, the two-structure paradigm of "mobile" ministry (apostles, prophets, and evangelists) and "settled" ministry (elders and deacons) began to give way to the settled component.[8] By the second century, early church father Ignatius of Antioch writes regularly of local church bodies having one pastor (at this time also called a bishop), a body of elders (presbyters), and a group of deacons. By the year AD 200, the term *priest* was being applied to clergy.

One of the main reasons for this consolidation was the perceived need to respond to heresy and division that had started to spread due to lack of institutional control. Judaizers maintained that Christians must adhere to Jewish customs and laws, while Docetists taught that Jesus' human nature was not real. In response, the bishop Ignatius of Antioch wrote letters directing a focus on the tighter leadership and structure of local churches.[9]

As a result, by the late third century the church had developed a sophisticated organizational structure. In Rome alone, Eusebius reported "one bishop, forty-six presbyters, seven deacons, seven subdeacons, forty-two acolytes, fifty-two exorcists, readers, and doorkeepers, and over fifteen hundred widows and needy persons." In addition, Rome became not just the seat of imperial power, but a center of church authority. Contrary to the loose structure of the early church, local churches solidified their organizational structures and became part of "*the* church," which convened a Council at Nicaea—the first of over a dozen over the ensuing centuries—in AD 325 to determine right (and wrong) doctrine. By this time there was also no mention of prophets or teachers in the writings of the Church Fathers, perhaps because those functions were fulfilled by the local bishop and presbyters.[10]

In AD 313, Roman Emperor Constantine issued the Edict of Milan, declaring tolerance for Christianity throughout the empire. Suddenly the church went from suspected outsider and persecuted enemy to favored establishment. Not coincidentally, this led to the further consolidation of authority within the church, as Christians no longer had to operate underground in fear of persecution.

MONASTICISM

When we think of monks, we may picture men in coarse brown cloaks or nuns in their black-and-white habits, cloistered together away from society and culture. Or maybe we picture a hermit, living by themselves in the desert or perhaps in a dark and drafty stone chamber. The reality, however, is much different. Historically, monasticism could be considered the first appearance of what we now refer to as the parachurch and was one of the most significant such institutions in the life of the church for more than a millennium.

It's true that the father of monasticism, Anthony of Egypt, was a hermit, or "solitary." Born into wealth in Alexandria, young Anthony heard Jesus' words to the rich young man that he should sell all he had and give to the poor (Mt 19:21). Anthony felt the words were meant for him personally, spurring him to give up his inheritance and retreat into a desert cave around AD 270, where he lived for nearly fifteen years in complete solitude, followed by another twenty years in self-imposed solitary confinement in an abandoned Roman fort. His goal was to be absorbed in communion with God, although people ended up flocking to him because of his wisdom. Others followed, leading to loose-knit desert communities. Many of these hermits moved to the wilderness in response to what they felt was the increasing secularization of the church in the era of Constantine.

Around the year AD 320, a former Roman soldier named Pachomius, also from Egypt, gathered these "desert fathers" into a community to form the first Christian monastery. For each of the communities he formed—seven for men and two for women—Pachomius established a common "rule" that governed participants' shared life, including meals, labor, and worship.[11] Benedict of Nursia (Italy) further systematized monasticism, instituting his famous Rule, which, in addition to governing the community's shared life, stated that all guests to the monastery should be received as Christ.[12]

As monastic communities developed, they became extremely beneficial to both the church and the world. "In the fourth, fifth and sixth centuries, and in medieval Christianity both East and West, nothing was more vital to Christian life than monasticism," writes historian Robert Louis Wilken.[13] Within the monastery they translated Scripture and preserved the writings of the church fathers,[14] while outside their walls they were integral to the life of the surrounding community. For example, Benedict insisted that his monks learn to read and write,[15] an opportunity that had previously been limited to clergy. From this sprang forth rudimentary community schools that Charlemagne later mandated within every monastery.

In addition to forming schools, monasteries provided employment for domestic servants, including "attorneys, physicians, goldsmiths, masons, and plumbers."[16] Rural monasteries in the high Middle Ages became agricultural producers, while some were involved in iron and coal mining.[17] Through these endeavors, monasteries contributed to the financial, spiritual, and even geographical improvements of their surrounding towns and cities. In many cases, monasteries *created* the villages, so central were they to local socioeconomic development.

Monasteries were also the forerunners of modern hospitals. In the late fourth century, Basil of Caesarea purposed to build a new kind of Christian monastery, one that focused on the physical care of the sick and poor. Basil's complex outside Caesarea included "residential medical facilities for the sick staffed with nurses and physicians, living space for the elderly and infirm, a hostel for travelers, a hospice for lepers who had been driven from the city because of disfigurement, a church, and a monastery."[18] These services were provided free of charge. In addition to providing care, monasteries and their new hospitals de-stigmatized illness and elevated compassion for the sick and infirm.

Monasticism ebbed and flowed. The monasteries and those within them, like any institution, were subject to the temptations and abuses that come with institutionalism, namely, the accumulation of wealth and power. As a result, reform movements would spring up within and outside of existing monasteries: the Trappists were formed as a reform to the Cistercians, who themselves were a reform movement within the Benedictines. The Franciscans were founded as a traveling mendicant order in the early thirteenth century by Francis of Assisi. Eschewing wealth, Franciscans traveled through the mountains of Italy, preaching and caring for the poor.

The rise of universities in the late twelfth century shifted intellectual leadership away from cloisters,[19] and during the

Protestant Reformation, Martin Luther—himself a former Augustinian monk, now married to a former Cistercian nun—declared war on the monasteries. King Henry VIII of England followed suit as part of the English Reformation. The destruction was swift. By 1540, all monasteries and abbeys in England were gone.[20]

Lay involvement. It must be noted that monasticism, at least for its first eight hundred years, was largely a *lay* movement.[21] Like the early apostles, the men and women who formed or joined monastic orders did so because they felt led by the Holy Spirit. As the church became more institutionalized and leadership opportunities more limited, monasticism provided lay women and men opportunities for service and mission. Many orders created associations of "confraters" or "tertiaries" by which lay men and women could participate in some of the prayers and other activities of the order.[22] Pious lay church members, known as circles of "friends," provided additional financial support for monasteries and abbeys, while the laity also served as a source of new recruits.

Monasticism was especially beneficial for women. Although the number of nuns and abbeys was much smaller, female branches of male orders provided opportunities for women "to step free of inherited roles and expectations and opened up new vocations in the church and society."[23]

Relationship to the church. The relationship between monasticism and the church was often complicated. During the monastic period, local churches and their clergy were needed to say mass, hear confessions, and provide spiritual direction for nonordained monastics. However, monastics were viewed as a drain on time, personnel, and diocesan finances. As a result, clerical dioceses and monasteries of ordained monks were reluctant to take on responsibility for nonordained monastic communities, especially when they felt these communities did not provide any spiritual benefits to them in return. While monastics often felt opposition from secular clergy, the feeling was mutual, and many monastics held an anticlerical stance.

Then there were questions of authority, not just with the church but among fellow monks of different orders. Conflicts over jurisdiction sometimes caused splits and led to the formation of new religious communities. Since most monastic communities were comprised of and supported privately by laity, it wasn't clear who had formal authority over them. At the same time, new religious groups wanted ideological legitimation and financial support from the church hierarchy.[24] It didn't help that there were some forty-four popes in the ninth and tenth centuries alone, with an average reign of less than five years each.[25]

A prime example of these conflicts over authority can be seen in the story of the Waldensians, an ascetic lay movement formed by Peter Waldo in the late twelfth century. Waldo and his followers preached that apostolic poverty was the way to perfection. In addition to his questionable teaching, "Waldo was convinced that the Scriptures commanded him to preach to the poor with or without bishops' approval."[26] In 1184 the Waldensians were declared heretical—not because of their message, but because they were not willing to recognize the authority of local bishops regarding the content of their preaching and recognized standards about who was qualified to preach.

Meanwhile, in 1210 Pope Gregory gave papal recognition to the order of Francis of Assisi, finally bringing monasticism under the auspices and authority of the church. Two years later, the Fourth Lateran Council declared an end to the creation of new orders "lest too great a variety of religious orders leads to grave confusion in God's church."[27]

Impact. Despite its ebbs, flows, and tensions, the influence of monasticism on Christianity, both formationally and missionally, cannot be overstated. For more than seven hundred years, the monastery was the center not only of culture and civilization, but also of mission.[28] In addition to its impact during its peak era, monasticism blazed a trail for the coexistence of institutional and external ministry structures. It also laid the foundation for the work of many of today's parachurch organizations, including evangelism, healthcare, preaching, ministry to the poor, and education.

MIDDLE AGES

While the early and high Middle Ages saw a flourishing of monasticism, the end of this period also gave rise to the first universities. Until this time, "cathedral schools" (large churches of the bishops) trained parish priests. These were eventually opened to laypeople and soon attracted foreign scholars.

In 1088, a group of foreign students in Bologna, Italy, banded together and hired scholars from existing lay and church schools to instruct them in the liberal arts, law, and theology. These smaller "schools" then joined together to form a larger association: the university, or "whole body of people." In 1158 the Holy Roman Emperor Frederick I Barbarossa issued a charter for the official establishment of the university as a center for the study of civil and canon (or church) law.[29]

Universities soon sprang up around western Europe. The University of Paris emerged from the Cathedral School at Notre Dame via royal charter in 1200; the University of Oxford in 1248. By the fifteenth century there were more than seventy universities in western Christendom alone, along with the first university in the Americas in 1553, in Mexico City.[30] Of course, all of this activity was regulated by the pope. Indeed, education became a chief focus of the Catholic Church; the Jesuits, formed by Ignatius Loyola in the early sixteenth century, set about creating a network of Catholic schools and universities in Europe and beyond.[31]

The Middle Ages also brought a new emphasis on Bible translation. For nearly a millennium, the church had utilized the Vulgate, a Latin translation of Scripture. Englishman and Oxford professor John Wycliffe, deeply concerned about false teachings and practices in the organized church, advocated that the Bible be translated into the then-common Middle English so that even the "humble ploughboy should be able to read the holy scriptures and understand what God would say to him." Although Wycliffe himself did not translate the entire Bible into English, his advocacy for translation into vernacular language led to the Wycliffe Bible and lives on through the contemporary translation organization that bears his name.

Little did anyone know that the church was on the cusp of revolutionary change initiated by a German priest and theology professor, a former Augustinian monk named Martin Luther.

4

HOW DID WE GET HERE?

CHURCH AND PARACHURCH IN THE
PROTESTANT TRADITION

Before the Reformation there was not a Catholic Church in the Roman Catholic sense we think of today. It was just the church. There were no denominations. There was one central authority, the pope. (Unless you count the time from 1378 to 1408 when there were two popes, and the time from 1409 to 1417 when there were three popes, but those are stories for another time.) The Protestant Reformation, inaugurated when Martin Luther nailed his ninety-five theses to the door of a church in Wittenberg, Germany, in 1517, sent shock waves throughout Christendom. Luther and his fellow reformers shaped the church—and what eventually became known as the parachurch—in ways they may not have intended or anticipated.

First, the Reformation led to the end of monasticism within Protestantism. Protestant princes in Germany, Austria, and Hungary withdrew ecclesial status from cloisters and abbeys, ordered them closed, and confiscated their property.

Unfortunately, in so doing "the Reformers had denied themselves a very important missionary agency," writes David Bosch. "It would take centuries before anything remotely as competent and effective as the monastic missionary movement would develop in Protestantism."[1]

Just like the Catholic Church did before them, Protestants took tight control of all ecclesial structures and activities. Of course, the reasons for this were obvious at the time: the future of the church was at stake in what was often a literal life-and-death battle. Unfortunately, the focus on doctrinal purity and purging led to significant declines in charitable and evangelistic work, particularly efforts led by laity. "If there was any talk about mission (which there usually was not), only the institutional church could act as sending agency."[2]

Second, Martin Luther effectively became the first Christian publisher. Others such as Jan Hus had preached similar ideas as much as a century earlier, and the printing press was invented in 1436, long before Luther's ninety-five theses. However, Luther uniquely understood the power of the printing press to spread his ideas and turned Wittenberg into one of the largest publishing centers in Germany. From 1502 to 1516, printers published an average of eight books per year. Over the next thirty years, by contrast, publishers in Wittenberg put out an average of *ninety-one* books per year, for a total of at least 2,721 works. One in three were Luther's own works, while another 20 percent were those of his Wittenberg colleagues—a staggering output in that day.[3]

ENLIGHTENMENT

The Reformation had scarcely died down when another era arose—the age of Enlightenment. Treaties such as the 1555 Peace of Augsburg and the 1648 Treaty of Westphalia allowed the coexistence of more than one religion in a country or region. Reform movements such as Pietism, Puritanism, and Methodism led to the creation of even more religious groups, although they would not be called "denominations" until about 1740.[4] Nowhere was this truer than in the American colonies, where European church traditions, ethnic loyalties, sectarianism, and American free enterprise combined to form a uniquely pluralistic religious society.[5]

The Enlightenment also birthed the revolutionary concept of the privatization of religion—that is, that religion was a personal and not a state matter, and individuals could choose their *own* religious affiliation. Religious toleration was even a founding principle of the United States. This concept of "voluntarism" meant that women and men could choose their religion, their denomination, their church, and eventually, their other voluntary affiliations, such as parachurch organizations and where they donated their money and other resources.

The positive outcome of this was the new flourishing of what were then known as "voluntary societies." The negative outcome was that religion, Christianity included, eventually became unintentionally consumeristic.

NEW WORLDS

The Enlightenment overlapped with the end of the Age of Exploration, during which European nations began exploring the rest of the world. While much of this exploration was exploitative, it also led to increased Christian concern for the spiritual and physical well-being of people in other lands. In Catholicism, these efforts took the form of global mission work by the Jesuits. In Protestantism, this took the form of the first "voluntary societies" that were created for specific purposes. These included British organizations such as the Company for the Propagation of the Gospel in New England—focused on Native Americans (est. 1649)—the Society for the Propagation of the Gospel in Foreign Parts (SPC, 1701), and the Society for Propagating Christian Knowledge (SPCK, 1709).[6]

The SPG and the SPCK were founded by English clergyman Thomas Bray, who had previously established libraries in America and England and helped to establish the Church of England in Maryland. Bray's organizational plan for the SPG and SPCK included a vision "for a corporate body empowered to receive gifts and legacies, and charged both to send missionaries to the plantations, provide them with libraries, and care for the maintenance of themselves and their dependents."[7] Incredibly, both organizations are still active today, and Bray is rightly considered the first multi-organization founder within the parachurch sector.

Between 1670 and 1770, Britain established itself as a global power, replacing the declining Dutch Republic through a series of military victories and expansions in Asia, the Americas, Spain, and France. Shortly after, the North American colonies declared independence from Great Britain, although the two countries remained inseparably linked economically, politically, and spiritually.

GREAT AWAKENINGS

The First Great Awakening swept across Great Britain and the nascent colonies in the 1730s and 1740s, bringing an emphasis on personal piety and devotion. The Second Great Awakening, from the 1790s to the 1830s, brought not only personal revival and greater church attendance, but also increased fervor for social reform in areas including abolition, temperance, prison reform, child labor laws, workers' rights, housing reform, women's suffrage, concern for the poor and marginalized, and educational opportunities for women, freed slaves, and children.[8] This enthusiasm manifested itself in an explosion of new voluntary societies.

One of the first such societies in Britain was the London Mission Society, founded in 1795. At around the same time, a group of prominent men who lived near each other in the village of Clapham, just south of London, began to gather regularly to discuss the societal problems of the day and what they could do about them. Led by William Wilberforce, the "Clapham Sect" led the fight against slavery and helped found a journal, *The Christian Observer,* as well as a number of missionary and tract societies, including the Church Missionary Society, the British and Foreign Bible Society, the Society for Bettering the Condition of the Poor, and the Society for the Reformation of Prison Discipline.[9]

The fervor soon crossed the Atlantic. In just a few decades, the list of voluntary societies in the United States included the American Bible Society (founded 1816), the American Sunday School Union (1817), the Young Men's Christian Association (1851), and the Women's Christian Temperance Union (1874), among dozens of others—many of which are still in operation today. Astonishingly, these efforts were funded almost exclusively by laypeople. As historian Kenneth Scott Latourette notes, "Never had any other set of ideas, religious or secular, been propagated over so wide an area by so many professional agents maintained by the unconstrained donations of so many millions of individuals."[10]

Where were local churches and denominations in all this activity? At that time, the local church was seen as a center for worship and administration of the sacraments. Denominations were collections of churches, generally not yet operating their own agencies for evangelism or social concern. Their work consisted primarily of church business on the local and diocesan levels, although that business also included the preparation of clergy through denominational universities such as Yale and Princeton. Denominations actually utilized voluntary societies to conduct religious work outside of the local church.

However, in the 1840s a partnership between Presbyterians and Congregationalists known as the Plan of Union began to disintegrate. Those denominations and others began to form their own missionary agencies, publishing houses, and outreach organizations. In addition, new denominations proliferated at astonishing speed. The second half of the nineteenth century alone witnessed the formation of at least a dozen major new denominations.[11] But these changes were only a hint of what was to come in the next century.

TWENTIETH CENTURY

In 1901, the United States was still regionally isolated. Sixty percent of Americans lived in a rural setting. Less than fifty years later, the United States was a global power, its population was majority urban, and a host of innovations and inventions had permanently changed not only everyday life but the life and work of the church. American Christianity also experienced an explosion in parachurch organizations that we still feel today. What led to such cataclysmic changes?

Technology. At the dawn of the twentieth century, most people traveled by foot, by horse or horse-drawn carriage, or by rail. Life revolved around one's neighborhood. Churches were established in these neighborhoods, following the parish model of the Catholic Church. Near my house in an older, historically Dutch neighborhood of Denver, there used to be two Christian Reformed Churches within a few blocks of each other—and neither had a parking lot. People attended the church in their neighborhood, and they rarely moved away from their community or city.

A host of inventions radically changed this lifestyle, including the radio, the automobile, the airplane, the television, and feature-length motion pictures. These inventions—all introduced and adopted by millions of people within just a few decades—made the world more accessible, minimized regional dividing lines, created entire new industries, and gave rise to a new consumer-driven culture in which people could choose where to spend their income and increased leisure time. Instead of being confined to their neighborhood, people could drive to their grocery store, gas station, vacation destination— or church—of choice.

As in the past, Christians utilized new technologies to further the work of the gospel, forming new organizations around their purposes. Radio Bible Class, founded in 1938, was one of a number of organizations formed to harness the power of radio. Mission Aviation Fellowship (1945) and JAARS (formerly Jungle and Aviation Radio Service, 1948) were formed to utilize airplanes to carry and support missionaries and to distribute Bibles and other Christian literature. The Billy Graham Evangelistic Association (1950) was originally formed as a media ministry, establishing World Wide Pictures as its motion-picture division in 1952. Billy Graham also founded *Christianity Today* magazine in 1956.

Society and culture. Two World Wars further hastened globalization and took American servicewomen and men even further from their homes. Even if a soldier, seaman, or military secretary had attended a local church in their home community, they were now displaced around the globe, far from their pastor or priest. A variety of ministries sprang up in response to the need for spiritual support for Christians scattered abroad. The Navigators, for example, took its name from its origins as a teaching and discipleship ministry to sailors in the US Navy. The post–World War II baby boom led to the rise of youth culture with the home losing its place as the center of society. Thanks to the G.I. Bill and an increasingly mobile society, more young adults than ever before went off to college, once again away from their families and home churches.

Parachurch organizations sprang up around the country to meet these needs. The locations of these organizations also testify to the growth and migration of the American population: Youth for Christ was founded in 1940 in New York by Jack Wyrtzen; Young Life was founded in 1941 in Texas by Jim Rayburn; and Campus Crusade for Christ (now Cru) was founded in 1951 in Southern California on the campus of UCLA by Bill and Vonette Bright.

Parachurch organizations were also aided by several important changes to the United States tax code. The Revenue Act of 1936 introduced the tax deduction for charitable contributions, making nonprofit organizations an appealing financial choice; the Revenue Act of 1943 instituted the requirement that nonprofit corporations file Form 990, stating their activities and financials; and the Revenue Act of 1954 established the modern tax code, including section (501)(c) for exempt organizations.[12] These changes brought stability and greater legitimacy to nonprofit corporations, including parachurch organizations.

Theology. But the parachurch landscape in the twentieth century was shaped not only by technological and cultural factors—it was also impacted by a significant theological shift at the end of the nineteenth century. For most of the 1800s, most American Christians held to a postmillennial theological perspective; that is, they believed that Christ would return after a lengthy period (a millennium, or one thousand years) of Christian influence and victory in society and culture. The belief that the millennium was at hand spurred evangelical

Christians to action around a host of social issues, as we have seen above.

However, the Civil War, lingering post-war national division, and the effects of rapid urbanization and industrialization called this optimism into question. Society seemed to be moving backward, not forward. In response, evangelicals shifted their theology to premillennialism: the idea that Jesus could come at any moment, *before* the millennium. This "theology of despair" exempted evangelicals from social concern,[13] and evangelical focus shifted instead to verbal evangelism for the purpose of saving souls before Christ returned.

Whatever postmillennial evangelical optimism remained was dealt a fatal blow by World War I. It was hard to believe that the world was growing in righteousness to precede the return of Christ when millions of men were being slaughtered in Europe. In addition, Randall Balmer explains, "The Scopes trial of 1925 convinced many evangelicals that American society had turned against them and their values." They responded by turning inward, "directing their considerable energies toward the construction of the evangelical subculture, a vast and interlocking network of congregations, Bible institutes, seminaries, camps, missionary societies and publishing houses."[14] Indeed, some of the best-known Christian organizations in the world began in the 1940s and 1950s, including AWANA, InterVarsity, Young Life, and Compassion International. My Christian college (Trinity International University) and seminary (Denver Seminary) were both founded in this era, as was the Christian camp (Fort Wilderness) where I worked after graduating from college.

The result of these factors—technology, society, culture, and theology—was an explosion of parachurch organizations, what sociologist Robert Wuthnow calls special purpose groups. He notes: "At the start of the twentieth century, denominations outnumbered special purpose groups two to one. By the mid 1970s, special purpose groups outnumbered denominations," leading to a radical restructuring of American religion.[15] This proliferation continues, with many new Christian nonprofit organizations of the late-twentieth century rising from nondenominational roots: think of missionary agencies such as Pioneers (1979), the Willow Creek Association (1991), the church-planting organization Acts 29 (1998), and of course, Promise Keepers (1990).

RISE OF THE MEGACHURCH

When Jerry White wrote his seminal book *The Church and the Parachurch: An Uneasy Marriage* in 1983, he could not have foreseen the biggest church-changing development of the last forty years: the rise of the megachurch. According to the Hartford Institute for Religion Research, a megachurch is a Protestant congregation that has an average weekly worship attendance of 2,000 or more members.[16] Although there have been very large churches over the course of church history, the megachurch is a distinct phenomenon of the mid- to late-twentieth century. Researcher Scott Thumma notes that "nearly all current megachurches were founded after 1955" but that their explosive growth began in the 1980s and did not slow for decades. Today there are more than 1,800 megachurches in the United States.[17] These include churches that meet in one location as well as multisite churches with multiple congregations meeting in different locations, including over the internet.

While the majority of megachurches are denominationally affiliated, they are functionally nondenominational, utilizing the parachurch sector for programs, publications, and seminaries[18] and offering so many of their own ministry programs that the megachurch itself becomes what White has termed "a federation of parachurch ministries."[19] Megachurches may operate their own food courts, bookstores, publishing arms, sports ministries, summer camps, car-repair ministries, radio and television stations, and food pantries. Some even act as sending agencies for their own missionaries.

The rise of the megachurch corresponded with a rise of a "non- or post-denominational Protestant identity."[20] In the mid-1950s, a Gallup poll showed that 96 percent of the adult population still affiliated with the faith tradition of their childhood. By 1995 denominational switching in adulthood was common, precipitated by factors including interfaith marriage, moving to a different town or neighborhood, dissatisfaction with one's church, or personal ties and influences.[21] If "nondenominational" were itself a denomination, it would now be one of the largest in the United States.

Even churches are downplaying their denominational affiliations. Sunday services often look very similar to the casual observer whether the church is denominational or nondenominational. It is not until you look "under the hood" that you find a church is affiliated with a denomination. Indeed, many churches have taken the denominational affiliation out of their name based on feedback that denominationalism is a turnoff to prospective visitors. Few people know that Saddleback Church in California was a member of the Southern Baptist Convention. Life.Church, based in Oklahoma City and pastored by Craig Groeschel, is a member of the Evangelical Covenant Church.

Interestingly, every jump in reported individual nondenominational affiliation has been accompanied by an increase in nonprofit incorporation filings, creating a two-way street. Parachurch organizations "are making it easier and more attractive for other congregations and individuals to go outside of denominational structures," writes sociologist Christopher Scheitle.[22] At the same time, Christians are increasingly viewing themselves as "just Christians," not hemmed in by denominational boundaries or even by church walls. They can choose from a plethora of organizations for religious programs, services, and opportunities to give of their time and money.

THE NEW CENTURY

The end of the twentieth century inaugurated explosive growth in internet services and technology, also known as the "dotcom boom." In the early 1990s, I got my first email address and checked for messages via a dial-up connection to the internet. In 1994, Jeff Bezos launched a new company called Amazon from his garage in Seattle. Seven years later, Steve Jobs of Apple Computer introduced the original iPod, promising 1,000 songs in our pockets. The first iPhone followed in 2007.

Churches and Christian ministries soon jumped on the tech train, designing websites to provide information about their work and using email to communicate with constituents. As internet capability increased dramatically, ministries were able to provide audio and then video content, first via stored content and then livestreamed. Meanwhile, the emergence of blogging allowed anyone, organization or individual, to publish their own content.

The first decade of the new century introduced social media, podcasting, and YouTube to the world. Once again, churches and ministry organizations, not to mention individual believers, suddenly had dozens of ways to communicate with friends and "followers." You could even attend church without leaving the comforts of home.

Technology has bridged distances and fostered connection in many ways, at least virtually. Missionary communication, for example, has been revolutionized by the internet. Ministry organizations can share their work to a much broader audience, quicker than ever before. Donors and volunteers can easily connect with opportunities to share their gifts and can see immediately where those gifts are having an impact. Shut-ins can watch church worship services online. Populations that may have once been marginalized from the mainstream of ministry have found places to serve and to speak up and out. And of course, technology was a literal lifesaver for many people during the pandemic, when there were significant restrictions on in-person gatherings.

The rise of what is known as the "digital economy" has also led to what is termed the "attention economy," in which success is defined by how many people engage with your content. This has fostered even greater competition in all sectors, including

Christian ministries, for people's eyes and ears. We are just now beginning to see the longer-term effects of a steady diet of digital consumption, and Christian leaders need to wrestle earnestly with not just the positive benefits of technology but also the detrimental effects to human souls.

ROMAN CATHOLICISM

After losing centuries of influence thanks to its rejection of modernism, in the mid-sixties Pope John XXIII convened a Catholic ecumenical council in part to "open the windows of the Church in order to let in some fresh air."[23] One of the resulting documents from Vatican II, as it became known, was a "Decree on the Apostolate of the Laity," which stated that the needs of the times demanded that laypeople be given more responsibility and opportunity to share the faith and work for "the prosperity of the family, culture, economic matters, the arts and professions, the laws of the political community, [and] international relations."[24] The church was declared to be a movement more than an institution, a "sign and instrument" of the kingdom of God. Fellowship and collaboration with "dialogue partners" from other religions was encouraged.

Indeed, this goal of Vatican II has come to fruition. Today there are far more lay ministers than diocesan priests. In addition, the openness to interfaith dialogue helped lead to the historic 1995 *Evangelicals and Catholics Together: Toward a Common Mission*, jointly edited by evangelical leader Charles Colson and Catholic priest Richard John Neuhaus. While some conservative Christians believe cooperation is not possible without doctrinal agreement, the book demonstrates the continued dismantling of historical boundaries, especially in the parachurch sector.

CONCLUSIONS

What can we learn from this overview of what we now commonly refer to as the parachurch? I'd like to suggest five takeaways.

The gospel always comes to people in historical robes.[25] Christians of each period in history understand and experience their faith in different ways than believers of other eras.[26] The history of the parachurch is a history of response to the needs and issues of the time, using the technologies of the time. Monasticism was originally a response to the perceived secularization of the church. Universities formed out of the rise of scholasticism. Martin Luther fomented reform with the printing press. The voluntary societies of the nineteenth century were driven to ameliorate social ills exacerbated by increased urbanization. The explosion of twentieth-century parachurch organizations was spurred by the perception that society was turning against evangelicals. And megachurches responded to—and capitalized on—a mobile, suburban, technology-driven society to create regional ministry centers.

God can use anyone, at any time, for any purpose. Parachurch-like movements and ministries have been started throughout history by men and women, young and old, wealthy and poor, educated and uneducated. Some have been embraced by the institutional church, others resisted or even openly opposed. Yet the truth remains: God's Spirit blows wherever it wishes (Jn 3:8, CEB). It is not confined within the walls of the institutional church or by denominational or doctrinal differences.

Throughout history the parachurch has largely been a lay phenomenon. Regular men and women with no designs on (or sometimes opportunities for) clerical ministry within a local church have gone on to start global movements and international organizations. The laity have also served as the foundation for funding and volunteer service for these organizations. The parachurch sector has been particularly enabling and empowering for women. Dating back to the monastic societies founded by Pachomius, the parachurch has provided space for women to teach, preach, pastor, and lead when the institutional church has met them with closed doors. Indeed, most of my own life my calling to vocational ministry has been—has sometimes *had to be*—pursued within parachurch organizations including camps, youth ministries, and higher education institutions rather than the institutional church.

Parachurch organizations can bring diverse Christians together over a shared mission or ministry. There is no doubt that non-denominationalism in the parachurch sector and in the church has brought Christians together across historically deep divides. Presbyterians can study the Bible and enjoy fellowship with Catholics in Bible Study Fellowship. Methodists and Moravians swing hammers side-by-side for Habitat for Humanity. Reformed and Arminian are equally welcome in InterVarsity. I have heard that Southeast Christian Church, a megachurch in Louisville, Kentucky, has jokingly been called the biggest Lutheran, Methodist, *and* Baptist church in the city because of its diverse membership.

Misunderstandings and outright tensions between the church and the parachurch and their respective roles in the life of the individual Christian are nothing new. Medieval monasteries competed with the established church for resources and legitimacy. In 1215, the Fourth Lateran Council stated that tithes to the local church took precedence over all other financial commitments. In the fourteenth century, John Wycliffe criticized the church for its excessive wealth and hierarchical structures. And in 1995, "the United Methodist General Board of Discipleship issued a warning that Promise Keepers was 'not in keeping with United Methodist theology and practice.'"[27]

The three dominant perspectives on these issues, held stridently by their proponents, have been and continue to be:

1. The institutional church (primarily in its local expression) is most important and must be central.

2. The institutional church is inflexible to accomplish the ministry being provided by parachurch expressions.

3. People don't even *need* established forms of the church; all that matters is personal piety and relationship with Christ.

In the next chapter, we will begin to address these perspectives and try to resolve some of the church-parachurch tensions by looking for a shared understanding in answer to the key question: "What is the church?"

5

WHAT IS THE CHURCH?

THE MEANING AND MARKS OF THE CHURCH

A few years ago, I helped convene the first of what has become an annual gathering of church and parachurch[1] leaders who are interested in furthering conversation and partnership. At that first invitation-only event, thirty women and men converged in Denver from around the United States. These leaders represented local congregations, national church networks, and national and global Christian nonprofits focused on everything from orphan care to church planting to publishing to worldwide evangelism. After listening to Dr. Jerry White describe a picture of the current church/parachurch landscape, it was my turn to take the music stand[2] to lead a session on "Biblical and Theological Foundations." I began by asking participants to write their answer to this question: "What is the church?"

I had a hunch how this might go, and that hunch was confirmed as I wandered among the tables while most participants struggled to answer my question. Pens hovered above paper, brows furrowed, sighs were uttered. Eventually, folks began to scratch some thoughts. After a period of somewhat uncomfortable working silence, I asked people to share what they had written. While there were some bullet points and common themes shared across the room, very few people were able to succinctly answer my question. A number expressed that the exercise was much harder than they would have expected.

I then asked participants to write their answer to a second question: "What is the parachurch?" Again, a similar response. A few concepts, but even fewer clear answers or definitions. More head scratching, but this time I also caught a few glances that seemed to represent glints from possible lightbulb moments.

Finally, I asked each person to put to paper a graphic model—using words, images, or a combination—that represented how they understood the relationship *between* the church and the parachurch. Once again, most participants struggled to articulate a clear conception of this relationship, especially one that incorporated their answers to my first two questions. Let me remind you that these were national and global *leaders* in the church and parachurch. But again, I was not surprised thanks to an experience I had years earlier.

I was in a room with another group of ministry leaders, this time a collection of students in a graduate-level ministry leadership class I was teaching. I had served as a ministry leader in a variety of organizational contexts for more than twenty years. That experience, along with master's and doctoral degrees in ministry leadership, now qualified me to teach this eager group of adult learners gathered in a classroom near Washington, DC.

I was teaching "ministry" and "leadership" as I had learned it, for the "church" as I had learned it. The class was rolling along like normal, and then as I was mid-talk, standing in the middle of the U-shaped arrangement of tables, I had a sudden realization—actually, more an out-of-body experience—that stopped me cold. *I'm teaching to a particular model of ministry,* I realized, *and I don't know how we got to this model, or if I even buy this model.*

Let me tell you: realizing that you perhaps don't buy into the things you are teaching, that you are even building your professional career on, can be pretty jarring. And then I had a follow-up realization.

I've been a Christian for nearly thirty-five years and a member of local churches all my life. I've been in professional ministry for more than twenty years. I have a bachelor's degree in ministry from a well-known Christian college, a master's degree in ministry from a respected seminary, even a PhD in ministry leadership from THE *Southern Baptist Theological Seminary—and I know way more about leadership than I do about the church.*

For the first time in decades of education, hands-on ministry, writing, and teaching, it struck me that this fact was a problem. *And* I was pretty sure that I was not the only one with this problem.

My aha moment in that classroom years ago led me on a journey to learn about the church: not how to manage it better, but to understand its identity, nature, and role in God's redemptive work in the world—and by extension, to better understand *my* identity and role as a member of this body.

What is this . . . this *thing* . . . that God established millennia ago, of which we as followers of Christ are now a part?

What I have learned has literally changed the course of my life, both personally and professionally. My goal now is to do my best to "champion the church," to raise this awareness in my work with other leaders. We can't afford to *not* understand the church. Not just as some "out-there" entity, organization, or institution, but as *ourselves*. We, the church. It's a matter of identity and our responsibilities in light of that identity.

So, what is the church?

No, really: I'm posing to you the same question that I asked that group of church and parachurch leaders. I want you to grab paper and pencil or your computer or your phone and start thinking and writing:

What is the church?

WHAT'S IN A NAME?

"Loaded terms" are words or phrases that carry strong emotional meaning and, therefore, color the use of the word for the user or the hearer. I constantly preach to my students the importance of clarifying exactly what they mean when they use words that can have loaded meaning.

For example, consider the word *biblical*. For each of us, that word carries significant meaning, usually tied to the very foundations of our faith. Yet when we use the word *biblical*, we are always referring to *a particular interpretation of the Bible*, and that interpretation is *always* colored by our personal experience, by our current cultural context, and by how heavily we weight tradition in our interpretation.

We may use or hear phrases such as a "biblical worldview" or a "biblical perspective on politics," but the meaning of *biblical* depends entirely on who is using that word. "Biblical" can mean completely different things to a progressive mainline Christian and to a conservative evangelical—and differing understandings of "biblical" have literally changed the course of history. It's a loaded term. Other common loaded terms in Christian circles these days include *gospel*, *evangelical*, and *deconstruction*, to name just a few.[3]

I contend that the word *church* is another loaded term. Not only have we assigned different meanings to this word, but many people hold very strong opinions and emotions about their chosen meaning. Think about the multiple meanings we have assigned to the word *church*:

- A particular congregation (e.g., First Christian Reformed Church in Denver, Colorado)
- An organization that has regular worship gatherings at multiple sites or campuses (e.g., Seacoast Church, with fourteen campuses in South Carolina and online)
- A worship gathering or service (e.g., "I'm going to church on Sunday.")
- An organizational purveyor of religious experiences or services (e.g., "Come to Christmas Eve at First Baptist Church.")
- A denomination (e.g., The Southern Baptist Church, the United Methodist Church, the United Church of Christ)
- The Roman Catholic Church (e.g., "The Church")

- Any group of believers gathered together (e.g., "My Bible study group is my church.")

- A brand that is used to market resources and expertise

- Any activity that seems to foster an individual's perceived experience of closeness to God (e.g., "I have church when I go hiking in nature.")

- The physical building in which a congregation gathers (e.g., "We'll meet at the church and take a bus to the youth retreat.")

- All Christians around the world (i.e., "the big C" or "universal" church)

- Any gathering that includes at least one Christian and any type of spiritual component (e.g., a "Beer and the Bible" group that meets at the neighborhood pub each week or a hiking group that prays at the end of its hike)

Complicating matters even further, most of us use the word *church* in multiple ways. I regularly use it in at least five of the ways I've listed above.

But can church truly be all of these things? I don't think so. In fact, I'd like to challenge us by borrowing the famous line from Inigo Montoya in the movie *The Princess Bride*: "You keep using that word, but I do not think it means what you think it means."

THE ECCLESIOLOGY PROJECT

Several years ago, my husband and I commissioned a mixed-methods research project conducted by Springtide Research to learn what people believe about the nature and purpose of church. Not surprisingly, the research revealed a wide variety of perspectives. Regarding the primary purpose of church, interviewees responded:

[The purpose of the church is] bringing community together, uplifting others spiritually. I think people should get a better understanding of their beliefs from the church that they choose to attend. I think they should have a feeling of hopefulness and uplifting by being amongst their peers and their spiritual guidance counselors.

The primary purpose of the church is to worship God; anything else is secondary now. There's some really good secondaries, like to evangelize. And then there are all the things that we find in the Book of Acts and the New Testament Church about orphans and widows and needy and all that, and the group condition. So those are all really good, really important things.

I think of [church] as a way to practice faith and become a part of community. That's a big part of it is being with others. But I feel like the purpose of it, the goal of it, is to be with others in and as a community together practicing the faith.

Some people go to church just to shout and listen to the pastor huff and puff and take it to the mountain top. But that's not what it's about. [Church] should be a learning place to take care of your family, biblically, how to handle your money, or anything dealing with day-to-day life, like how to treat your spouse.

While many respondents felt that it was important to gather regularly and in-person for worship and community, others

WHAT IS THE CHURCH?

felt that this type of experience is not necessary to build a relationship with God.

"I don't feel guilty because church is in my heart!"

"I don't go to church because I can talk to God anywhere."

"I believe if I pray at home, the church is not necessary."

"I carry my faith everywhere I go and pray wherever I go."

"I do not believe going to church is any more faithful than not going to church."

Note again the differing understandings of the word *church*. To some it's a building, to some it's a gathering, to some it's a spiritual experience. Even for those who believed it was important to gather regularly, their understanding of the purpose of that gathering ranged from worship to evangelism to gaining hope to receiving practical guidance for living out their faith.

As to how people came to their understandings of church, a majority derived their beliefs from their upbringing—by either accepting or rejecting what they had been taught and experienced as they were growing up. In keeping with historical and sociocultural trends, most respondents grew up going to church with some regularity, as part of families and a larger society that valued involvement in a local congregation.

But as we saw in chapter two, today the United States and much of the Western world is post-church, de-churched, or unchurched. I believe this makes it even more important for us to discuss the question, "What is the church?"

Since there is such a lack of clarity today about this thing called "church" and because a clear understanding is so critical to both our membership and our ministry as followers of

70

Christ, in this chapter I'm going to lead us on an exploration of ecclesiology, or a theology of the nature, purpose, and structure of the Christian church.

A lot of what I will share in the pages ahead has come from my own journey as a result of those a-ha moments in my classroom years ago, when I realized how little I really understood about the church. At that time, I could articulate a "systematic" ecclesiology in order to write a passing paper for a professor. I also had a "functional" or "working" ecclesiology that had been shaped by my experiences growing up and as a ministry leader. But I had never dug deep enough to be able to articulate an integrated understanding of the church from theology to practice.

Perhaps you're in a similar situation, or perhaps you feel like you already have it all figured out. Either way, I encourage you to read with an open mind. I know that my own thinking was challenged and changed as a result of my earnest exploration. We'll begin our journey by looking at what the Bible says before panning to larger theological themes, the influence of historical tradition, and current sociocultural realities.

THE ASSEMBLY

The word translated "church" in our English Bibles comes from the Greek word *ekklēsia*, which means "assembly." *Ekklēsia* was a common term, used for hundreds of years before the Christian era to refer to an assembly of persons who were part of a well-defined membership such as a group of citizens.[4] For example, the Septuagint (the Greek Old Testament) uses the word to describe assemblies of the Israelites (Deut 4:10; 9:10; 31:30).

The word was first used in the New Testament in Matthew 16:18 when Jesus foretold the establishment of the church, and then again in Matthew 18:17 in Jesus' instructions for dealing with sin in the church. Although *ekklēsia* only appears these two times in the Gospels, Luke uses it twenty-three times in the book of Acts and Paul forty-six times in his letters, including twenty-two in 1 Corinthians.[5] Of 114 total uses of the word *ekklēsia* in the New Testament, 109 refer to Christian assemblies.[6]

Catch that: throughout the majority of the New Testament, the "church" refers to *local assemblies of Christian believers*.

It has become fashionable these days to talk of the dominance of the "big C church" ("Church") or the "universal church."[7] It is true that the apostle Paul and the writer of Hebrews speak of the idea of the church consisting of all believers across time and space (1 Cor 12:12-14; Eph 5:23; Phil 3:20; Heb 12:22-24). However, the theological concept of the "invisible church" was introduced by Clement of Alexandria, nearly two hundred years after the birth of the church. Similarly, the term *universal* church finds its origins not in the Bible or from the apostles or the earliest believers, but from the Catholic Church in the fifth and sixth centuries, during which several popes began to refer to the *ecclesia universalis*, meaning the church (at that time, there was only one institutional "church") throughout the world as a whole.[8]

But make no mistake, the *ekklēsia* referred to in the New Testament had "its location, existence, and being within definable geographical limits."[9] The "universal" or "global" church, therefore, refers to believers in the collection of these embodied gatherings, not simply to the totality of *individual* believers around the globe. When I refer to any sense of the global church ("the" church) throughout the rest of this book, it is within this understanding of all believers around the world *as they are connected in local communities*.

In addition, "church" in the Bible almost always refers to the people who gather, not to the building or location in which they gather. As Earl Radmacher writes, "The union with Christ is invisible, but the church is always composed of people."[10] And the true church consists of *believers*.

Note the last word of that last sentence. The *ekklēsia* in Scripture refers to an assembly of *Christians:* a "gathering of believers" or "group of those who trust in Christ."[11] When Luke writes in Acts that over three thousand individuals were "added to their number," he explains that they became part of the church not by simply gathering to hear Peter, but by believing what Peter said and by being baptized—in other words, by becoming Christians. That doesn't mean that nonbelievers were (or should be) excluded from joining the assembly, but the *ekklēsia* consists of those who follow Christ: the congregation of God.[12]

Okay, hold on for a minute.

Perhaps you feel your temperature rising at what I just wrote. The church as a local gathering of believers?! What about reaching nonbelievers? And what about reaching outside the walls of the church? What about evangelism, social justice, meeting the needs in our communities, cities, and around the world?

If we are to be true to the biblical texts, we need to concede that "church" as described in the New Testament *(ekklēsia)* was understood primarily as local assemblies of believers who gathered regularly. While each of these gatherings is a complete church with spiritual and heavenly significance, the collection of assemblies constituted the one *ekklēsia*. In other words, "In God's purpose there is only one church, one gathering of all under the headship of Christ. But on earth it is pluriform, seen wherever two or three gather in his name."[13]

Activities and marks of the church. The New Testament writers also tell us what those earliest believers *did* when they gathered. According to Acts 2:42, "They devoted themselves to the apostles' teaching and to fellowship, to the breaking of bread and to prayer." Paul elaborates in his first letter to the Corinthians, describing their assemblies as including "a hymn, or a word of instruction, a revelation, a tongue or an interpretation" (1 Cor 14:26). In other words, the earliest church gatherings included worship, preaching, and edification.

The question arises as to whether all of this is simply *descriptive* or intended to be *prescriptive* for all congregational gatherings, for all time. The answer to that depends on your view of Scripture and its authority, as well as on the weight that you give to tradition, to *which* tradition, and to that tradition's interpretation of Scripture.

Meanwhile, the idea of a "congregation" implies an interactive membership,[14] and according to Acts, the believers "had everything in common" (2:44) and met together for meals (2:46). Indeed, the earliest churches were known for their love for one another and demonstrated an "intensive, interactive common life."[15]

As Mark Dever writes,

> Much of the material in the [New Testament] letters represents the working out of this common life, as the authors encouraged believers to interact in such a way that both brings glory to God and reflects their shared status as Christ's followers, Christ's disciples, and Christ's friends.[16]

That writing includes more than thirty "one anothers" in the New Testament that are to mark believers' interactions. Simply stated, the church was and is a fellowship, and "the Christian life can be fully realized only in relationship to others."[17]

Biblical metaphors for the church. This idea of the church as a fellowship can also be seen in the primary imagery in Scripture of the church as Christ's body (Rom 12:4-5; 1 Cor 10:16-17; 12:12-27; Eph 1:22-23; 5:23, 30; Col 3:15) with Christ as its head (Eph 5:23). Because believers were all baptized by one Spirit into one body (1 Cor 12:13), commitment to one another was essential. We often think of the parts of the body in terms of the use of spiritual gifts in service, but our membership in the body of Christ is primarily relational, not functional. "The church is not a what, it's a *who*."[18]

A secondary image is that of the church as a household or family (Heb 3:1-6). Paul frequently refers to fellow believers as his brothers and sisters, while John writes to "little children" (1 Jn 3:18). Since family relationships are maintained by members behaving appropriately to one another, Paul often exhorts members of God's family to proper behavior (1 Tim 3:15; Gal 6:10).

The Bible also describes the church as a flock being cared for and guided by shepherds (Jn 21:15-17; Acts 20:28-30; 1 Pet 5:2-4), the bride of Christ (Eph 5:25-33), a temple for God's Spirit (1 Cor 3:10-17), and a royal priesthood (1 Pet 2:5-10). In all of these, it is clear that there is a spiritual dynamic to the church that goes beyond its earthly functions. There is something supernatural, a sacred significance that happens when Christians gathers around and in Christ.

So the church is a community. But in addition to their activities during their gatherings and their behaviors with one another, Scripture also tells us what the believers did *outside* their assemblies. Acts 2:45 says that they "sold property and possessions to give to anyone who had need." They gave regularly in proportion to their income, sending that money to other churches (1 Cor 16:1-3; 2 Cor 8:1-9:15; Rom 15:14-32). They were driven to live out the teachings and practices of Jesus toward the least and the lost. In other words, the earliest churches were marked by a sense of mission. In fact, God's mission is foundational to the church. However, *mission* is another loaded term that will require some unpacking.

6

WHAT DOES THE CHURCH DO?

THE MISSION AND MINIMUMS OF THE CHURCH

What comes to mind when you hear the word *mission*? For many years, I associated that word exclusively with "missionaries"—and in particular, with *foreign* missionaries, men and women who had been called to other countries, for a particular type of work: to evangelize and make Christian converts.

Over time, my understanding of missionary work and the word *mission* broadened to include not only foreign missions, but also evangelistic work in the United States. Then it expanded even further to include not just conversion evangelism, but a host of other types of gospel ministry including caring for the poor, helping to heal the sick, and advocating for justice for the oppressed.

For some, the word *mission* may have connotations ranging from the crusades to colonialism to campus ministry to church planting to organizational mission statements, and those associations may be accompanied by strong emotion. It is definitely a loaded term. A lot has been done—both very good and very, very bad—in the name of mission. The word has been appropriated for a variety of purposes throughout history from the local church to far-off lands. Therefore, it's crucial that we come to agreement on what we mean when we talk about mission as it pertains to the church.

To answer this question I turn to the late South African theologian and missiologist David Bosch, whose seminal book *Transforming Mission: Paradigm Shifts in the Theology of Mission* scrupulously examines the concept of *mission* and traces the evolution of the understanding of the term throughout Christian history. His definition? "Mission means serving, healing, and reconciling a divided, wounded humanity."[1] This is far broader than just evangelism or conversion. It is all-encompassing redemption, and it is rooted in the very nature of God.

As Bosch writes, "Mission has its origin in the heart of God. God is a fountain of sending love. This is the deepest source of mission. It is impossible to penetrate deeper still; there is mission because God loves people."[2] And because God loves people, his mission is to reconcile humanity to himself. The mission of God, or *missio Dei*, is rooted in "our understanding of God as a missionary God, and the Bible as a missionary storyline, a storyline that is embedded in God himself saving mankind."[3] It is "God's turning to the world in respect of creation, care, redemption, and consummation."[4] And this salvation includes not only conversion of souls, but "the termination of poverty, discrimination, illness, demon possession, sin, and so forth."[5] It is a broad gospel.

Missio Dei is a Latin term that was historically used regarding the doctrine of the Trinity to explain God's sending nature: the Father sends the Son, and the Father and the Son send the Holy Spirit. But to this, we must add another movement: Father, Son, and Holy Spirit sending the church into the world. Mission is a movement from God to the world, and the church is an instrument for that mission. Mission is not merely an activity of the church; it is the expression of the "very being of the church."[6]

Notice the correct ordering of the relationship between the *missio Dei* and the church. The mission comes first, and the church exists because of that mission. The church is not the origin or center of mission; it is the fulfillment of God's mission. The church exists for the world. As Bosch notes, "It is the *world* God loves and for the sake of which the Christian community is called to be the salt and the light."[7]

On earth the church represents the kingdom of God—his rule, reign, and redemption. As Fran Blomberg writes:

> The church is a creation of God for the display of his victory over the powers of sin and death, a community of those called to his purposes, and evidence of his promise to completely renew creation. . . . Through its practices and actions the church represents the present kingdom as a gathering of those united and forgiven by God against all the odds of human prejudice and vengefulness.[8]

In fact, Jesus promises the "keys of the kingdom" to the church in Matthew 16:19. "Whatever he precisely means by this," Mark Dever notes, "the power of the kingdom is certainly being entrusted to the church."[9]

Remember, by "church" I mean *we* as the gathered people of God, not some vague institutional entity, or even the clergy. You and I, yet not as individuals: as members of a local congregation, the *ekklēsia,* the church.

Folks, I was decades into my Christian life and ministry—*decades!*—before I realized any of this.

Growing up, church was simply a place I went to and that others should "come to" as well. It was preaching and programs and fellowship. If there was any sense of "mission," it was either undertaken by specially called, super-spiritual missionaries who were sent into the world, or it was conducted *within* church walls and led by professional pastors and staff who were paid to do this type of thing. Furthermore, it was almost exclusively evangelistic, focused on "saving souls."

But friends, as members of the body of Christ we are *all* participants in God's mission to reconcile the world to himself. And so we proclaim the gospel not only by preaching the Word, but also by healing the sick, providing for the poor, and fighting for justice—and not exclusively to the ends of the earth, but to our neighbors next door. This biblical understanding of mission (just read the Gospel of Luke or the book of Acts!)[10] is far broader than mere conversionism. The church exists for the sake of the world, not vice versa.

I have no doubt that most of us would agree with all of this in theological principle. But if you look at our *functional* theology, the way most of us actually *do* church, you'll see that we primarily define church by what happens within its walls, particularly on Sunday mornings, with an emphasis on preaching and musical worship bookended by fellowship before and after.

When we engage in mission that isn't cross-cultural, our activities and budgets reveal the belief that mission happens primarily by coming to our buildings and programs and that it's the work of professional ministers, not an essential part of everyday discipleship by everyday believers.

It's time for us to reclaim a broad biblical understanding of mission and the church's core missional identity. But we also need to get the order right: "It is not the church that has a mission of salvation to fulfill in the world; it is the mission of the Son and the Spirit through the Father that includes the church."[11] And we can't fulfill the *missio Dei* through individual mission and service divorced from the *ekklēsia*.

Yet all of this is not to say that mission must exclusively originate from or be overseen by the institutional local church. Missionary bands took the gospel throughout the known world without formal orders from or accountability to a particular congregation. This apostolic function and structure will get special attention in the next chapter of this book when we look more closely at what is now often called the parachurch.

SOCIOCULTURAL VERSUS SPIRITUAL REALITIES

One of the most basic ways in which human beings organize themselves is through social groups. In this type of group, members interact with one another and are joined by some kind of principle which gives the group its sense of identity. For example, a recreational softball team is a social group.

Social groups can be further classified into two categories: kinship groups and non-kinship groups. A kinship group, as the name implies, is identified by a familial relationship and is the most basic, universal form of human belonging.[12] Non-kinship groups may contain kinship relationships but are not formed around them. Non-kinship groups may be formally or informally conceived and joined voluntarily or involuntarily, making them the broadest category of social group.

The formal organization is one type of non-kinship group, formed when people organize around what is called a "super-ordinate goal": a goal "that is so difficult, time-consuming, and complex that it is beyond the capacity of one person."[13] Formal organizations give meaning to people's lives because of the bonding that occurs over the organization's goals, and in the shared pursuit of those goals.[14]

Looking through a sociological lens, it would be easy to describe the church as a formal organization: a group of people gathered around a superordinate goal. In addition, in the eyes of the United States and many other world governments, the local church is considered a legal entity governed by various statutes and codes. However, we miss the mark—badly—to think of the church as just another formal organization.

For starters, the church is not a non-kinship group. It is a *spiritual kinship* group, bonded by the brotherhood and sisterhood of believers in Christ. In addition, the church is neither a project nor an organization conceived of by human minds and hands, nor is it simply a voluntary society such as those described in the previous chapter.

Rather, in the words of Edward Klink III, "The church is special—a sacred, special-grace institution that belongs entirely to God."[15] It is a divine institution because of the necessary connection between the Lord Jesus Christ and his body, the church. No other organization—nonprofits, government, or even families—has been so divinely established or connected. "It looks like other, common human institutions," says Klink, "but from God's word we know that it is actually a divine institution, created, sustained, and directed by God, with Christ as the senior pastor."[16] In other words, the church is an embodied spiritual entity, and there is something unique that happens in and through—and can *only* happen in and through—the *ekklēsia*.[17]

This may be a hard truth to swallow, especially for Westerners and Americans in particular. Our emphasis on the power of human direction ("leadership") indicates that we often view the church as just another earthly organization, not a truly divine institution whose existence is rooted in the missional nature of the Trinity, and which is referred to multiple times in Scripture as the very bride of Christ.

SHAPED BY HISTORY AND TRADITION

Within an easy walking loop from my house I can encounter a Russian Orthodox church, a Greek Orthodox church, a Reformed Catholic church, a local campus of a multisite nondenominational congregation, a Lutheran church, a Roman Catholic church, a Seventh-Day Adventist church, a United Methodist church, a Baptist church, several nondenominational church plants, and a network of house churches. If what I've outlined here describes the biblical underpinnings and theological nature of the church, how have we ended up with so many perspectives and understandings of church, many of them significantly different if not completely incompatible with one another?

To be honest, in one sense it's a wonder that there is *any* unity. Over the course of two thousand years of church history, in a faith that spans the globe, there have been a multitude of branches and splits: some of them major, some seemingly minor but no less significant in terms of impact over time. Many of these were intended as course corrections to perceived errors in belief or practice. Over time, new reform movements sprang up to reform the movements that themselves had been earlier attempts at reformation. *Ecclesia semper reformanda est*—Latin for "the church must always be reformed," often shortened to *semper reformanda*, or "always reforming"—can be a viewed as a feature, not a bug, of the community of Christ.

However, this brings us to where we are today, with wide variations in understandings and practice of "church." As I mentioned earlier, there are multiple factors that inform our understanding and resulting practice. The primary one is our view of the role and authority of Scripture, especially *vis-à-vis* tradition, experience, and reason. Is the Bible the sole authority for faith and practice or do the other elements have any place? When Scripture talks about the church, is it prescriptive or simply descriptive? If it is primarily descriptive, how much flexibility and freedom do we have to create or change structures and practices, and who gets to decide? We can look at any expression of "church" today and find clues that help us ascertain what mixture has shaped that expression.

An almost unlimited number of combinations results in an almost unlimited number of expressions of church. You'll find people meeting in house churches, folks who meet for church over Zoom, others who attend services in ornate cathedrals, and everything in-between. So, too, the practices within those gatherings can vary greatly. An online church might follow the ancient rhythms of the church calendar and the liturgy. A service in a cathedral might feature contemporary praise and worship songs and a sermon preached by a pastor in jeans instead of a clerical robe. Leadership and decision-making structures can vary from a simple congregational structure to the vast hierarchy of the Roman Catholic Church.

Most importantly, the variety of combinations has resulted in foundational differences in understanding the foundational nature and purpose of church. Cardinal Avery Dulles has condensed these into five different models or visions for the Church.[18] These include:

1. **The Church as Institution.** This model emphasizes the internal structure and governing order of the church as a "perfect society" whose permanence was established by God.

2. **The Church as Mystical Communion.** In this view the emphasis is on the church as a community not only "horizontally" with fellow humans but also "vertically" in communion with Christ as a representation of Trinitarian relationship.[19]

3. **The Church as Sacrament.** According to this model, the church is a sign and instrument of the presence of

Christ in the world, calling the world to cooperation and fellowship. This view attempts to unite the Institutional and Mystical Communion views.

4. **The Church as Herald.** This model holds that the church is gathered and formed by the Word of God.[20] Sacrament is secondary. The church's role is that of proclamation of the Word of God to the world.

5. **The Church as Servant.** In this vision, the church exists not to gain new members, but to serve the world by putting the words of the gospel into action and working for social justice.

The reality is that each of these models finds strong support in Scripture, and the church should in some ways reflect *all* of them. However, most of us strongly favor only one or (maybe) two of them. Our model for the church then guides our everyday practice.

I grew up in a Protestant Evangelicalism that viewed the church as Herald. I didn't know any other visions for the church existed. The model I learned, primarily by immersion, was simply "the" way. It wasn't until much later that I began to understand the existence and merit of the other visions. And each of us carries these same types of assumptions, often subconsciously. Is it any surprise that we have trouble coming to agreement?

ECCLESIAL MINIMUMS

So is there a "right" way or a single definition of *church*? I've been reflecting on this question for years, ever since my classroom epiphany. What makes something a church—an *ekklēsia*—today? What are the "ecclesial minimums," the basic requirements to be considered a church?

Not far from my house, an old church building has become home to the International Church of Cannabis. Is this a church? What about a Bible study group? A hiking club that talks about God and prays together? A chapel service at a Christian college? A concert by a famous worship artist? A liturgical service in Latin at a famous cathedral?

Is a church a "church" because of where and how it gathers? Because of what it does during those gatherings? Its activities outside formal gatherings? Because of who is part of the gathering? How its people treat one another within the congregation? How they interact with the world? Because of what they believe? Because of some mystical or theological characteristics?

The Protestant Reformer John Calvin held that the church existed wherever "the Word of God was purely preached and heard, and the sacraments administered according to Christ's institution."[21] Meanwhile, the contemporary missional church movement holds that the church exists wherever worship, community, and mission overlap.[22]

Here are how some others have attempted to define church:

- "The church is a community of people whose life is derived from the life of God."[23]

- "The church is a witnessing community of the people of God."[24]

- "A local church is a faithful, formal community of Christians who gather for the purpose of meeting God in his word, praying to him, praising him, building up each other in the faith, building unbelievers into the faith, loving one another, and managing the affairs of the church."[25]

■ "The church is the community of God's people, functioning as the agent of God's kingdom, promoting the expansion of God's economy, all for God's glory."[26]

■ "The church is fundamentally a local community of believers who band together under a designated leadership structure for fellowship, teaching, worship, and outreach to the lost."[27]

■ "The church is the people of God who have been saved through repentance and faith in Jesus Christ and have been incorporated into his body through baptism with the Holy Spirit. This universal church becomes manifested in local churches characterized by being doxological, logocentric, pneumadynamic, covenantal, confessional, missional, and spatio-temporal/eschatological."[28]

■ "The church is a community of people gathered around following Jesus and participating as agents of restoration in the reconciliation of all things."[29]

I believe an effective definition must consider the biblical and theological nature of the church, which is then exemplified in certain *prescriptive* purposes and practices. A foundational definition must also be flexible enough to allow for different *descriptive* forms derived from different theological streams, historical understandings, and contemporary contexts while remaining true to the church's biblical essence.

Based on those qualifications and my reading of Scripture, I would like to propose the following understanding of church:

The church (biblical *ekklēsia*) is the divinely established, called out, and sent collection of all the people of God around the world, animated and united by the work of Christ and guided by the Holy Spirit, who gather regularly in locally embodied community to re-center their lives around God and who seek to live out kingdom values in their relationships with one another and with the world.

Whew, that's a mouthful. Let me unpack this definition piece by piece:

- **Biblical:** I'm not looking at understandings that developed over time, such as the models described by Avery Dulles. I am trying to find explicit biblical foundations and prescriptions.

- ***Ekklēsia*:** The word in the Greek New Testament that is now translated "church."

- **Divinely established:** See Matthew 16:18. The church was instituted by God, not created by humans.

- **Called out:** The church is comprised of believers who are called to live differently, to be holy.

- **Sent:** The church is sent by God to the world as the embodiment of the *missio Dei* (Jn 20:21, Acts 1:8).

- **Collection of all the people of God:** The true church is comprised of those who have committed to the lordship of Christ.

- **Around the world:** The church consists of all believers regardless of geographic location.

- **Animated and united by the work of Christ:** Christ is and must always be at the center of the church and must motivate our every thought, word, and deed. In addition, the church is one in and with Christ as his body and bride.

- **Guided by the Holy Spirit:** Human leadership must ultimately be guided by the Holy Spirit, not by our own agendas.

- **Who gather regularly:** The when, where, and how often are not specified, but Hebrews 10:25 instructs believers to not forsake gathering together.

- **In locally:** The biblical understanding of *ekklēsia* primarily refers to geographically situated congregations.

- **Embodied:** This is the adjective that might get me the most pushback, given the rise of exclusively online environments and communities. However, I believe that Christ's incarnation and the nature of humanity point to the significance of embodiment—of an *in-person* relational experience. Just as I think most of us would say that a marriage cannot be realized entirely online, I believe that true participatory community must have some type of embodied element.

- **Community:** The church is marked by commitment to one another versus merely consuming content or services together. There is a sharedness, a common life and mission.

- **To re-center their lives around God:** This can be accomplished via various means and has taken different shapes in different streams: musical worship, the sacraments, the Lord's Supper, prayer (both talking to and listening to God), reading and preaching the Word of God, and other components of the liturgy.

- **And who seek:** There is an intentionality, an active desire.

- **To live out:** "Being the church" is not only an individual, internal state of being. It is exercised in our words and actions.

- **Kingdom values:** The church as agent of the kingdom must be marked by the king's values including restoration, redemption, compassion, justice, mercy, forgiveness, and many others as seen in Scripture.

- **In their relationships:** Again, the body of Christ is a *who* of humans, not an institutional *what*.

- **With one another:** As fellow members of Christ's body, we are commanded to relate to each other in certain ways. (See again all the "one anothers" in the Bible.) In addition, the world will know we are Christians by our love for one another (Jn 13:35).

- **And with the world:** The mission of God is directed at the whole world, the *entirety* of humanity, not just at believers.

Well, there you have it.

Take a few moments to reflect on each component. What do you think? How does your understanding differ from what I have presented here?

Keep in mind that just because I don't use your exact language in my definition doesn't mean it's not there. Various denominations and theological streams will flavor or interpret parts of this in their own way.

Then go back toward the beginning of this chapter and look at the numerous contemporary understandings of *church* that I described. Based on what we've explored and what I have attempted to define, which ones might we cross out as inaccurate?

You can certainly adopt my understanding, but I encourage you to clarify your own. It won't bother me one bit if you come up with a different definition. My real intent with my definition is to provide a springboard for your own reflection. It's imperative that we understand the church because it is central to our identity as followers of Christ. We also need to understand what the church *is* to understand what it is *not*. And these understandings must be grounded in biblical reality, not just in our personal experiences or preferences.

Now, what if you took your definition (or mine) seriously? What if we truly believed the church was all of these things? What if we actually lived as members of a called out, sent, intentional, God-centered, Holy-Spirit-guided, Christ-united, kingdom-living, world-loving, relational community?

Read those again. Imagine with me for a moment.

Wow.

So, let's keep working to clarify our ecclesiology.

7

WHERE DO WE STAND WITH ONE ANOTHER?

MAPPING THE CHURCH/PARACHURCH TERRAIN

In the summer of 1979, four years before Jerry White's *The Church and the Parachurch* was released, *Eternity* magazine ("The magazine for committed Christians, applying all of God's Word to all of life") splashed this provocative question on the cover of its June issue: ARE CHRISTIAN ORGANIZATIONS MUSCLING OUT THE CHURCH? The accompanying cover graphic displayed a man's bare, muscled arm tattooed with the logos of well-known Christian organizations including the Billy Graham Evangelistic Association, Youth For Christ, the Christian Broadcasting Network, and others.

The cover was a teaser for a feature article titled, "The Great Evangelical Power Shift: How has the mushrooming of parachurch organizations changed the church?" The author of the article (and *Eternity's* editor) Stephen Board began by pointing out, "Just as there are paramedics, paralegals, paratroopers—each meaning 'alongside' something else—so there are para-*church* movements that work alongside conventional churches."[1]

Board continued:

As these organizations have grown, the clergy and church leaders have wondered if the tail has begun wagging the dog. In influence and money—that is, in *power*—the parachurch agencies are running away with the ballgame. Their critics, usually pastors, charge them with imbalance, doctrinal difference, and exploitation of congregations for money and people. The major criticism, and one that is easiest to make stick, is that they lack accountability to anyone but themselves. Parachurch groups are religion gone free enterprise.[2]

Was Board's article accurate? Is it still true today? Most importantly, if what Board wrote was and is correct, is that a bad thing?

WHAT'S IN A NAME?

Our first task is to define what we mean by *parachurch*. Interestingly, it's not clear when that term was first used. Perhaps Board coined the term in his article for *Eternity*. The authors of *The Prospering Parachurch* suggest that it became popular in the late 1960s, but no one seems to know for sure and my research did not reveal a definitive answer. At any rate, *parachurch* has become an accepted term for a concept that also goes by many other names.

"Voluntary societies" organized around specific purposes were hugely influential in the United States and the United Kingdom from the mid-seventeenth century. Before that (and continuing today) the Catholic Church featured monastic orders supported by confraternities or tertiaries. Today, their parachurch descendants could also be called voluntary associations, religious nonprofits, faith-based organizations, or special purpose groups or organizations, the latter of which is the term used by social scientists.

In many countries, these special purpose groups are considered nonprofit organizations—meaning not that they are restricted from making a profit, but that those profits must not be paid out to private shareholders or individuals.[3] In addition, many nonprofits are also classified by government tax codes as "tax-exempt" organizations, meaning their income is exempt from certain types of taxes. Different countries have different classifications, but again these are governmental designations. In the United States, the most familiar entity is the 501(c)3 organization, which must be organized and operated specifically for approved tax-exempt purposes, including (among others) charitable, religious, or educational purposes. Other countries have similar designations for charitable and/ or nonprofit organizations.

To confuse matters further, however, not all parachurch organizations are charitable organizations or nonprofits. For example, for decades the California-based Youth Specialties— an organization that supported youth ministers through conferences, training events, and published resources—was a for-profit corporation that netted its individual owners a small fortune in profits. (YS is now a subsidiary of the nonprofit Youth Ministry Collaborative.) In addition, most Christian publishers and bookstores are for-profit organizations whose products benefit members of the church at large but which do not necessarily consider themselves to be "parachurch."

What all of these types of organizations do have in common is a specific and explicit Christian organizational mission: what author Joann Keyton refers to as a "superordinate goal," or a goal that cannot be accomplished by one person alone.[4] That mission can focus on a particular activity or a specific demographic group; it could be as broad as global evangelization or as narrow as a ministry to drag racers and their pit crews. The size and geographic focus of an organization's work can also vary widely. Some well-known organizations employ thousands of people, have a presence around the globe, and report revenue in excess of one billion dollars. Others may have a lone paid staff member or be run exclusively by volunteers, have an annual budget of less than $25,000, and feature a mission so specific or local that you will probably never hear of them.

Meanwhile we still don't have a clear definition of the parachurch. In a 1981 article for *Christianity Today*, J. Alan Youngren described the parachurch as a "not-for-profit, organized Christian ministry to spiritual, mental, and physical needs, working outside denominational control."[5] *Parachurch* is described in the *Dictionary of Christianity in America* as "voluntary, not-for-profit associations of Christians working outside denominational control to achieve some specific ministry or social service."[6] And Mikey Lynch defines *parachurch* as "organized Christian activity that is distinct from the visible, institutional church."[7]

In their book *The Prospering Parachurch*, Wesley K. Willmer, J. David Schmidt, and Martyn Smith draw from these definitions to suggest four litmus tests to delineate a parachurch organization:

1. Is the group organized as a nonprofit?
2. Does the group have a Christian mission statement?
3. Is the group independent of traditional church structures?
4. Does the group work at one or more specific ministries or services?[8]

While tests one and two are generally clear and reliable indicators, tests three and four can get tricky. For example, what about denominations themselves? Denominations can be large and highly complex systems with their own publishing houses, colleges and seminaries, missionary agencies, and social service and relief ministries. What about the variety of ministries that are run by or closely related to local churches, such as community development associations, or the constellation of ministries—bookstores, conferences, radio, television, and other media ministries—that fall under the umbrella of a large or well-known local church, its pastor, or its network?

Finally, what about organizations that may have had an initial focus on a specific ministry or service, but have evolved into something more general or something entirely different? The Christian and Missionary Alliance denomination began as a missionary sending agency before becoming a denomination. The reverse is also true, as many nonprofits begin within churches and are launched as independent nonprofits when they outgrow the church.[9] And there are college campus ministries that mimic local churches, with small groups, fellowship events, evangelism trips, and regular worship services that include preaching, baptism, and communion.

It's harder than we might think to nail down what we mean by what is often referred to as parachurch organizations. They are not automatically delineated by mission, size, scope, or geographic location, or even by tax-exempt or nonprofit status. Add to this the fact that many local churches also operate mission-driven programs or spinoff ministries, and defining the parachurch becomes as challenging as nailing Jell-O to a wall. At the very least, we must consider these organizations as part of a broad categorical umbrella that includes nonprofit organizations, Christian charities, and true "parachurch" ministries, with perhaps a few Christian mission-driven for-profit or public-benefit corporations as well. For now, though, I'll continue to use the term "parachurch" to refer to all of these organizations.

WHERE DO WE START?

When attempting to define the parachurch we need to determine our starting point, as that determines the direction of the conversation. Per popular definitions, "para" implies that the organization's work is done alongside the traditional church: the church is the point of reference with other organizations revolving around it. However, we must also once again clarify what we mean by the church. Is it the local congregation, a denomination, or the body of Christ made up of all believers?

If we hold to an understanding of church that emphasizes some type of regular gathering or congregation, then the "parachurch" designation should by definition require some type of connection to the congregation(s). But Christopher Scheitle points out, "The prefix 'para-' could be defined as something existing 'beside' or 'alongside' of a related entity. However, it could also be defined as something 'beyond' or 'aside from' a related entity. The difference is subtle, but it represents the crux of the problem."[10]

Jerry White has attempted to clarify terms by suggesting the term *parachurch* be replaced with "para-local church," which he defines as "any spiritual ministry whose organization is not under the control or authority of a local congregation."[11] White's definition and the others earlier in this chapter emphasize the locus of control between the church and parachurch, but I believe the primary issue is not *authority* but *centrality*. Where does a particular parachurch organization understand and place itself in relationship to the local church? And how does a local church view and live in relationship with parachurch organizations?

Again, in this understanding not all organizations categorized as parachurch are truly *para-church,* with an official relationship with a local church or group of churches. At best they may claim to serve—or serve as a branch of—the universal church.

White notes six theological perspectives regarding the "para-local church," depending on one's view of the centrality of the local church:

1. **Local church only.** This view judges any structure outside the local congregation as illegitimate. All mission

sending or other efforts must be under the direct authority of a local congregation.

2. **Temporary legitimacy.** This view believes that the local church is God's primary agency for ministry in the world. However, para-local church structures have been raised up for a *temporary* corrective influence on the local church. When the church begins meeting the need as it should, para-local church structures should disappear.

3. **Two structures.** In this view, the church consists of both local and mobile structures, with both having equal legitimacy in God's plan. The local congregation meets the growth needs of a body of believers, while the mobile structures perform missionary functions of evangelizing and discipling in the world.

4. **Church planting.** This view gives legitimacy to para-local church organizations as long as their goal is church planting. It is insufficient to perform a part of the function of a church if the direct result is not integration into an existing congregation or planting a new one.

5. **Dual legitimacy.** This view holds that both the local congregation and para-local church are legitimate expressions of God working in the body of Christ and permits a variety of structures in both branches. Since all are part of the broader body of Christ, individual believers, though part of a local congregation, express their ministry to the world in a variety of semi-autonomous structures. This differs from the two-structures view in that it allows for para-local agencies and non-missionary organizations.

6. Anti-institutional. This view looks upon the church in its institutions, organizations, and building as ineffective and unnecessary. It seeks nearly total freedom in individual expression with resistance to authority from either a local or para-local church.[12]

Looking at these six perspectives, which would most closely describe your view? How did you come to that understanding? In my experience and observation, most Christians today—myself included—have functionally grown up in a Dual Legitimacy world, with very little thought (or preaching/ teaching) given to the theological relationship between the local church and the parachurch[13] or the believer's role or relationship with either.

MODALITIES AND SODALITIES

One of the theological perspectives described by White is what is known as the "two-structure" paradigm. This view was first introduced in the early 1970s by Fuller Seminary missions scholar Ralph Winter. By looking at church history, Winter discerned two complementary structures, what he called the *modality* and the *sodality*.

The modality is "a structured fellowship in which there is no distinction of sex or age"—that is, a denomination or a local congregation. The sodality, on the other hand, is "a structured fellowship in which membership involves an adult second decision beyond modality membership" and whose membership is determined by common features such as age, sex, marital status, interests, or purpose[14]—such as missionary organizations following the precedent of the missionary bands seen in the New Testament. Other writers have described the two structures as the church "gathered" and the church "scattered" or "sent," the "left" and "right" feet of the church, the "stable" church and the "mobile" church, and "settlers" versus "pioneers."[15]

In Winter's view, the pre-Reformation Catholic Church with its local parishes (modalities) and monastic orders (sodalities) exemplified the ideal, albeit imperfectly executed, synthesis of the two structures. But as we saw earlier, Martin Luther dismantled the Catholic orders as part of his attempts to reform the church. "This [loss of a sodality structure], in my evaluation, represents the greatest error of the Reformation and the greatest weakness of the resulting Protestant tradition," Winter wrote.[16]

Winter and his protégés make the case that the local church was never designed to serve as the center or base for missionary activity. "Paul was 'sent off' not 'sent out' by the Antioch congregation," Winter noted. "He may have reported back to it but did not take orders from it. His mission band (sodality) had all the autonomy and authority of a 'traveling congregation.'"[17]

In addition, as Sam Metcalf argues, the local church *structures* are not conducive to apostolic (sent) ministry. "The church in its local, cross-generational, parish, diocesan form has never been—theologically, historically, sociologically, or missiologically—designed by God to cross barriers for the sake of the expansion of his kingdom."[18]

Metcalf, like his mentor Winter, points to the Roman Catholic Church as an example of the two structures operating together. "No one with a straight face would ever have called

Mother Teresa a 'para-Catholic,'" he writes.[19] Metcalf even suggests that "parachurch" is a "dirty word": "It needs to be exorcised from our vocabulary. There is really no such thing. Either we're part of the church or we're not. And as we've seen from the Bible and history, the church is not limited to its local form."[20]

To the two-structure proponents, the "big C" church has and should always consist of both the modality and the sodality. For scriptural support they point to Galatians 2:1-2 and 7-10 in which Paul wrote:

> Then after fourteen years, I went up again to Jerusalem, this time with Barnabas. I took Titus along also. I went in response to a revelation and, meeting privately with those esteemed as leaders, I presented to them the gospel that I preach among the Gentiles. . . . They recognized that I had been entrusted with the task of preaching the gospel to the uncircumcised, just as Peter had been to the circumcised. For God, who was at work in Peter as an apostle to the circumcised, was also at work in me as an apostle to the Gentiles. James, Cephas and John, those esteemed as pillars, gave me and Barnabas the right hand of fellowship when they recognized the grace given to me. They agreed that we should go to the Gentiles, and they to the circumcised. All they asked was that we should continue to remember the poor, the very thing I had been eager to do all along.

According to Bob Blincoe, a student of Winter's and the longtime president of Frontiers USA, in this passage "Paul and Peter shake hands, recognizing two administrations of the gospel."[21]

The two-structure paradigm sounds great. Its proponents make some compelling arguments. I love that they recognize the local church and its role. But I find some serious flaws with this paradigm as *the* model.

First, I don't believe the emphasis on structures has strong biblical support. The emphasis in Galatians is not on the structures by which Paul and Peter carried out their ministry, and even less on providing a prescriptive model. The two-structure model may have emerged from historical observation, but it does not stand up to exegetical scrutiny.

Second, the two-structure paradigm focuses primarily on missionary endeavors and does not consider the host of other types of parachurch or nonprofit organizations. (See White's descriptions of Dual Legitimacy vs. Two-Structure models earlier in this chapter.) Where does a Christian publisher fit into the two-structure model? What about a Christian camp? A Christian crisis pregnancy center?

Third, the model uses as an example the Roman Catholic Church. But even Mother Teresa waited many years for papal approval before beginning her ministry to the poor in India. In the Roman Catholic Church today, both modality and sodality are under a higher ecclesial authority. Post-Reformation Protestant Christianity does not have this type of central governing body, which is one reason there has been such a proliferation of parachurch organizations.

Fourth, denominations—while included as "modalities" in the two-structure paradigm—are far more complex, often containing sodality structures, including missionary sending agencies. The division is just not as neat as proponents of the model may desire.

Finally, while proponents of the two-structure paradigm assert that both the modality and sodality structures are equally "the church," this doesn't make sense in practice. As Mikey Lynch points out, "When this approach is worked out consistently, we have to say that every Christian actually participates in multiple churches of different sizes, often with overlapping leadership and membership."[22] All Christians are part of the body of Christ, but not all organizations with members of the body of Christ are the church.

While I believe the two-structure model falls short as an overarching paradigm, it paints a compelling picture of the advantages of apostolic flexibility and raises important questions about the effectiveness of institutional church structures. But is there a perspective that can hold space for both the church *and* the parachurch?

A FUNCTIONAL PERSPECTIVE

I believe that we have committed a fundamental error in the church-parachurch conversation by focusing on *structures* when the better (and, I believe, biblical) approach is to focus on *function*—in particular, the apostolic function.

The word *apostle* in our English Bible is translated from the Greek word *apostolos*, which appears more than eighty times in the New Testament.[23] *Apostolos* derives from the verb *apostellō*, which means "to send" and is used more than 112 times in the New Testament, including the following:

- Jesus is described as the sent one of God, primarily in the Gospel of John but also in the book of Hebrews.

- Jesus promised that the Father would send the Holy Spirit (Lk 24:49).

- During his earthly ministry, Jesus sent seventy-two believers and later his disciples, just as Jesus was sent by the Father (Lk 10:1-3; Jn 17:18).

- The word is most frequently used in the New Testament to describe "the apostolate"—the original group of twelve men, later including Paul, who were commissioned by Christ to preach, heal, and drive out demons, and who were accorded this office of authority within the early church because of their personal experience with Jesus and his ministry.

- Other men and women—as many as twenty-five different named individuals—are also characterized as "apostles" throughout the New Testament.

- The spiritual gift of apostle is described by Paul in his letters to the Corinthians and the church at Ephesus.

Today there are widely differing opinions about whether the office of apostle is still valid for contemporary times. Some believe that there are legitimate apostles today, just as there were in the New Testament. Others believe that the apostles were given only for the early church, and there is no equivalent office today.

Whatever you believe about the office of apostle, there is no scriptural evidence that the gift of apostle has ceased today. But I'm going to move beyond questions about the office and gift of apostle to contend that if we look at the whole of Scripture, the reality of God's sending nature—the *missio Dei*, which we looked at in the previous chapter—means that the *whole church* is sent.

The Nicene fathers agreed in AD 325 that the church's nature was "one, holy, catholic, and apostolic." At that time and for Protestants today, *catholic* meant "worldwide," while *apostolic* meant that the church's existence was rooted in the (original) apostles and in carrying what was entrusted to them by Jesus through continuous "apostolic succession" of leadership from those apostles.

Today, Protestants interpret *apostolic* to refer to a continuity of beliefs from the apostles and the traditions of the living church. However, I would argue that the church should also be apostolic in the "sent" sense that we see throughout Scripture, which is in keeping with the very heart of God.

The church—meaning the body of Christ, not just an institution—was created for mission. That mission includes not only evangelism and discipleship, but all types of gospel ministry: caring for those in material and financial need; advocating for justice; bringing healing to the physically, emotionally, and spiritually sick; and the list goes on. And that mission can and *must* be accomplished through a wide variety of activities, forms, and organizational structures. Taking the whole gospel to the whole world requires the whole church.

In Ralph Winter's framework, sodalities are comprised of "second decision" men and women who have felt a specific call to a missional vocation after the initial call to follow Christ, and beyond the reach of the local church. The world certainly needs those individuals. But I believe the second-decision terminology lets the rest of us off the hook. The reality is that as disciples of Christ, we are *all* sent—to the people next door, to our neighborhoods, our communities, our cities.

Within the last decade or so, a number of prominent missiologists have been calling the church back to its apostolic roots. Alan Hirsch argues that the words of the Nicene Creed should be reversed to apostolic, catholic, holy, and one, "so that apostolicity defines every aspect of the life and action of the church."[24] As Roland Allen wrote, "The Church was first established with a world-wide mission for a world-wide work."[25] And Edmund Clowney adds, "The body of Christ is working properly when each member is obediently sharing the good news of Jesus with the harassed and helpless (Mt 9:35-38; Lk 10:1; Rom 1:8, 10:14-18; 1 Thess 1:8)."[26]

And yet . . . the contemporary church is largely institution-focused, characterized and driven by "attractional" ministry and the leadership, teaching, and shepherding that happens within the church's walls. If apostolic mission was God's original design for the church, how did we get off track? Clayton Dye summarizes seven historical movements that have led to where we are today:

1. The first-generation church set the exemplary model of ecclesiology, empowering the apostolic gift with minimal ecclesiastical structures.
2. The rise of the bishop over the first fourteen centuries of the church eventually eroded leadership plurality, leading to a power struggle in ecclesiastical systems.

3. The Reformation brought back the importance of the authority of Scripture but also marked a loss of apostolic language and of the legitimacy of the ongoing, ordinary gift of apostles.

4. The First Great Awakening gave life back to the apostolic gift and set the stage for the rise of voluntary societies and of the modern missionary movement led by William Carey.

5. In the nineteenth century, a missional theology was developed, creating the need for the placement of the apostolic gift in ecclesiology.

6. The rise of the parachurch in the twentieth century gave validity to the ongoing, ordinary gift of apostles but left ambiguity about the relationship of the apostolic gift to ecclesial structures.

7. The church in the twenty-first century is rediscovering the language for the apostolic gift while the need for new ministry structures in a Post-Christendom culture is building momentum for the body of Christ to fully embrace the ongoing, ordinary gift of apostles.[27]

In other words, the stage is set, and it is time for us to reimagine what an apostolic church for the twenty-first century might look like. I believe that what we today call the parachurch is critical to that reimagined future, although I think we need to give it a different name. We'll get to that very soon.

The bottom line is that parachurch organizations are nothing new and they are here to stay. In fact, parachurch organizations today are deeply embedded into the cultural landscape, surpassing churches in recognition and impact. More than thirty-five years after Stephen Board sounded his alarm about the dominance of parachurch organizations, today they "have become the public face of Christianity in the United States and abroad."[28]

THE ADVANTAGES OF THE PARACHURCH

Parachurch entities have played a significant role in spreading the good news of Jesus Christ throughout the world, throughout history. We have seen them take shape in monastic movements, in voluntary societies, and in the form of many of today's well-known organizations. A quick look at these ministries reveals why. Parachurch organizations carry some significant advantages over a local church and for these reasons are a gift to the *ekklēsia*.

A primary advantage is *reach*. Because most parachurch organizations are not tied to a local church, they can operate in places a local church may not be able to access. Think of college campuses, military bases, refugee centers, and unreached people groups around the world. Specialized organizations can operate closer to front lines and reach further than locally bound congregations. Even this book about the church and parachurch will utilize the global reach of a (parachurch) publishing company.

In addition, some parachurch ministries fulfill roles that a local congregation never would or even should attempt to engage on its own: examples that come to mind include higher education, Bible translation, camp ministry, and publishing, among many others. And focused parachurch organizations can scale their efforts in ways that a generalist congregation never could. As Christopher Scheitle writes, "The characteristics of local congregations that make them ideal organizational structures for worship often make them less than ideal for outreach."[29]

A second advantage is impact thanks to *specialization*. Lesslie Newbigin has described three roles for the church: community, servant, and messenger.[30] A healthy local church will engage with all three of these roles, making it a generalist although it can never become an expert in all of them. Parachurch organizations, by contrast, are most effective when they focus on a single ministry and execute that ministry to near perfection. They are more efficient and able to quickly get resources to a specific need. Think of the impact of Compassion International and similar ministries, or of homeless shelters and food banks.

A third advantage that flows from the first two is opportunities for *lay involvement*. Most contemporary institutional church structures, led by recognized clergy and focused on ministry largely within or adjacent to their walls, cannot empower the priesthood of believers in the same way as the parachurch. Throughout church history, laymen and women have been discipled, trained, and released to ministry around the world through the parachurch sector. Many women, in particular, have found opportunities in the parachurch that they could not access in the local church.

By focusing on missional commonalities rather than theological differences, parachurch organizations demonstrate a fourth advantage: *promoting unity* in the body of Christ. Many parachurch entities are functionally interdenominational: for example, the work of Operation Christmas Child brings together Methodists, Lutherans, Catholics, Baptists, and all other flavors of the faith. I personally gained a much greater understanding of and appreciation for the breadth of the body by attending Campus Life as a teenager and making friends from multiple churches around my hometown.

Fifth and finally, parachurch organizations can help *call the local church to mission*. Apostolically focused organizations and individuals remind the local congregation of the needs beyond its walls and challenge believers to engage with those needs. Throughout history, parachurch organizations have provided needed correctives to mission drift and worldly entanglement by the *ekklēsia*.[31]

As Mikey Lynch summarizes:

> The best parachurches don't ultimately erode local churches and denominations, but enrich them. Through their ministries, there is greater zeal and maturity, more ministry competence, more theological depth, and more human beings saved from hell by the gospel of our Lord Jesus Christ. . . . Parachurch structures facilitate the full flourishing of God's saving work in the world.[32]

All this is to say that "parachurch" organizations are an essential part of the church and fulfill a number of critical roles in God's mission. They just operate differently. And now it's time to give them a new name.

REDEFINING TERMS

So, what should we call these ministries that are commonly referred to as the parachurch? As I wrote earlier in this chapter, the term *parachurch* implies that the (local) church is the point of reference. But the relationship is typically between the institutions or organizations, and some organizations are not meaningfully "para"-church. Meanwhile, the two-structure paradigm makes room for evangelistic and disciple-making parachurch organizations and their "second-decision" vocational staff but does not account for the broad range of other types of missional organizations or for significant involvement by the laity.

I agree with Sam Metcalf that we should get rid of the term *parachurch*, although for reasons different from what he articulates. Words matter, so it's important for us to consider, create, and begin using a term that more accurately encapsulates the unique nature of these entities.

Here is my suggestion: *missional extensions*.

Yes, I know it doesn't flow off the tongue as easily as "parachurch." It will take some explaining and some use over time to embed itself into our understanding and vernacular. But I think "missional extensions" is a far more accurate theological, functional, and organizational descriptor.

Theologically, "missional extensions" frames these individuals and organizations within the *missio Dei*. I am using "missional" broadly here to refer to the "sentness" of the body of Christ into all the world to meet all types of needs. For example, theological education is one mission. The publishing of Christian resources is another. So is caring for refugees, for orphans, for the poor; translating and distributing the Bible, providing hospitality for military families . . . we could go on and on. The needs and the missional opportunities are endless.

Along those lines, the term "missional extensions" reflects their functional focus: they are special-purpose entities, at their best when they are laser-focused on a particular aspect of mission for the kingdom. From an organizational perspective, the term gets rid of the institutional framework and communicates relationship in continuity: not side by side with walls between but as nodes on a global network, the whole church for the whole world in what Lynch refers to as a "gospel ecosystem."[33]

Let me note here that by putting the local gathering as the reference point, I am *not* saying that the local church must *control* all the other nodes. There is simply no biblical evidence that Jesus intended the "local church" to be the origin of all missional activity. Rather, I am suggesting that we lower the walls between the entities and allow free-flowing movement of monetary and human resources out and across the web of missional extensions, from local churches to the ends of the earth. The missional extension network includes individuals, local congregations, and other specialty ministries—but none of these operate on their own.

In the network, every individual serves as a missional extension in their place(s) of calling, whether that is around the corner, in their place of work, or an ocean away. But every individual believer is *also* connected to a local assembly, in keeping with the unique spiritual nature of the church that we examined earlier.

The *ekklēsia,* the local congregation, is most effective at what is called near-neighbor missionality and at gathering, worshiping, and growing in community. In these ways, local congregations should still be missional at their core. But external missional extensions can (as their name states) *extend* far beyond the reach of a single local community. Some assemblies might feel called to start their own missional extensions; that is perfectly acceptable, but other local assemblies can avail themselves of the advantages and opportunities of missional extensions ranging from the local food bank to the global evangelism agency. In this way, the church is broadly apostolic, both gathered *and* scattered, with each form playing a vital role in God's mission. This is not just Dual Legitimacy; it is dual *necessity.*

A paradigm shaped around a web of missional extensions also reduces "niche overlap," also known as "turf wars." Instead of clear boundary lines between organizations and their activities, we become true teammates playing on the same field. In fact, we *need* one another to function. If a node on the network fails, it can cause the entire network to break down. Or imagine an old-time string of Christmas lights: when one of the bulbs is taken away, all of the lights go out. What if we truly viewed every missional extension as a necessary node on the network? How would we help each other to prevent the entire network from going dark?

The apostle Paul did not have church and parachurch structures in mind when writing about the metaphor of the body in 1 Corinthians 12, but the principle that each part of the body of Christ is not just important but *necessary* can be applied to the concept of missional extensions:

> The mission org cannot say to the local church, I don't need you! The food pantry cannot say, because I am not a youth ministry, I am not part of the body. If the whole body were Habitat for Humanity, where would Denver Seminary be? Are all relief workers? Are all Bible translators? God has placed the church and parachurch together so that there should be no division, that they suffer together and rejoice together.[34]

Perhaps a new term and a new framework will begin to foster greater cooperation for the kingdom. For now though, the reality is that the church and missional extensions (i.e., the artist formerly known as the parachurch) still have trouble figuring out how to play together nicely.

8

WHY DON'T WE ALWAYS GET ALONG?

THE NEEDS AND CHALLENGES OF THE MULTIFACETED CHURCH

I am writing this over my Christmas break from work, having just made the turn into a new year. From my dining table near my front door, I can see a wicker basket overflowing with envelopes.

Just over a month ago I decided to collect every solicitation letter I received from missional extensions[1] before Christmas. Here in the United States, most nonprofit organizations receive the majority of their donations at the end of the calendar year because it is the deadline for making tax-deductible charitable contributions for that year. In addition, prospective donors are generally in a charitable mood around Christmas time. (Notice the order in which I listed these rationales. If we're honest, the Christmas spirit often takes a back seat to tax benefits.) Knowing this, most charitable organizations significantly ramp up their fundraising efforts during this period, leading to an influx of communication to my mailboxes, both email and snail mail, which in turn has led to the stack of envelopes in the basket by my front door.

Any guesses as to how many letters my husband and I received? Thirty-one, or just fewer than one per day. And that's just counting physical letters. That does not include email solicitations, social media ads and asks, personal requests, the requests at every cashier station at every store I visit, or the barrage of radio and television commercials during this season. Neither does it include the requests we received as part of Giving Tuesday, a global event created in 2012 to foster generosity and counter the retail mania and consumerism of Black Friday and Cyber Monday.

In addition, I counted only organizations that could be classified as missional extensions. I did not include the requests we received from not-explicitly-Christian nonprofits such as disaster relief agencies, disease awareness and research organizations, community services entities, performing arts companies, and the university I visited *one time* as a prospective graduate student in 2005 and which for some reason continues to send me *alumni* communication and solicitations, managing to track me down across three moves around the United States.[2]

Finally, my tally only included financial requests received over the last two months of the calendar year. We receive general requests at a fairly regular pace the rest of the year, with increased communication from any given organization when they are nearing the end of their fiscal year.

But the requests are not limited to the financial or the material. There are the requests to volunteer, to attend, to "support" this or that cause or organization by giving my time, my service, my presence. I work full-time at a missional extension (a seminary) and I belong to a local community of believers, which has its own missional programs and events. Then there are the multitude of other missional extensions around town seeking to meet the endless needs in our community and our city. I could serve at a food pantry, a homeless shelter, a secondhand store, a crisis pregnancy center, a local school.

Every missional extension (including the local church) rightly believes their cause is important, perhaps among the *most* important. To be fair, they *are* all important. Bible translation, campus ministry, children's sponsorship, refugee ministry, poverty alleviation, evangelism, theological education . . . we've already examined the myriad categories and efforts of these organizations. How do I choose between all of these legitimate needs?

Let's say I tried to prioritize the opportunities based on a particular area of interest or passion. I have a background in youth ministry, I have a heart for teenagers, and I want to focus my efforts locally, so maybe that would help narrow my options. But alas, even within that focus I could still give to and/ or serve at my local congregation or with one of at least a dozen area missional extensions focused on ministry to teenagers.

Why do I share all of this? Because my experience is symptomatic of the overlap, confusion, and sometimes tension that exists within the (well-intentioned) world of missional extensions that includes local congregations, nonprofit ministries, and everyday believers. On the one hand, I think it's fantastic that we have so many entities trying to meet so many needs. The world always needs *more* kingdom ministry, not less. On the other hand, a look at the big picture hints that we may have more of a mess on our hands than it may appear from any single perspective. In this chapter we'll take a closer look at the areas of the greatest confusion, conflict, and tension, the reasons behind them, and a proposed prescription for greater understanding and cooperation.

THE PRIMARY CHARGES

While the variety of Christian ministry entities generally claim to be on the same team, they are not always great teammates. At worst, there is outright criticism leveled at the historical "parachurch" by leaders of local congregations. Meanwhile, the harshest critics of the local church would say that external entities are needed because congregations haven't been doing their job in terms of missional ministry beyond their walls. Others would argue that external organizations are needed because local churches by design cannot provide the flexibility needed to foster and fulfill apostolic functions.[3] At the very least, many leaders of missional extensions express disappointment or frustration that local congregations aren't supportive (or more supportive) of their work and that there is no real partnership, or even attempts to that end.

THE UNDERLYING ISSUES

I believe there are four key issues underlying the lack of cooperation among ministry entities. The first is *practicality*. Intentional collaboration takes time and energy. Ministry leaders of all kinds and within all types of organizations are extremely busy. For pastors and church leaders, the saying goes, "Sunday comes every week." There are always sermons to prepare, worship services to plan, programs to organize and manage, congregational needs to pastor, and "parachurch" leaders are equally focused on their own ministries and the urgent needs inside and outside their organizations.

A second issue is *genuine differences*, either doctrinal or methodological. Two organizations may have the same mission but completely different views of how to get there, either in terms of external methods or internal/operational values. (Remember the concept of "loaded terms" from chapter five.) Cooperation, therefore, becomes much more difficult than we might think even when two parties have a similar missional goal. However, I believe we can often use this as an excuse to avoid the hard and messy work of collaboration.

The third issue is the reality of *free enterprise*, particularly in the United States. American parachurch history is firmly rooted in the American entrepreneurial mindset. If Christians see a need, they are compelled to meet it. This has been true throughout church history around the world, but it is even more true, more possible, and more celebrated within American Christianity.

However, this flexibility and freedom can be a tremendous strength while also bringing significant weaknesses and challenges. For starters, the entrepreneurial mindset coupled with the Western narratives of independence and self-sufficiency result in less collaboration. In communities and countries with great freedom, there is simply not a significant felt need for collaboration; in fact, it is often viewed as a sign of weakness. For example, I have noticed a greater degree of collaboration among ministries in my adopted city of Denver than I have experienced in other parts of the United States where I have lived and ministered, particularly in the South. While Colorado still holds strongly to a pioneering mindset, the harsh realities and loneliness of frontier life meant that cooperation was essential for survival, and that spirit remains to some extent today.

In addition, a free-market economy means that individual believers have the freedom to choose their involvements. Unlike countries in which there is a state church or greater religious restriction, the deeply rooted privatization and voluntarism of American religion allows each individual to customize their involvement from nearly unlimited options for worship, service, and giving. This means that local churches and other missional extensions must always be promoting their services and opportunities to potential participants and donors.

Churches and Christian ministries want to attract individuals who can choose but are sometimes resentful if they choose elsewhere. Even if someone does choose their organization, that commitment may not last. As a result, leaders can succumb to a scarcity mindset and even blame other organizations for encroaching on their "territory." There is no central authority in Protestantism to sort out any differences or disputes or to force parties to "play nice." But I believe these are just symptoms of a deeper issue.

The fourth and deepest issue is that of *unclear or bad models*. We have already explored the lack of clear understanding and paradigms for the church and other missional extensions. This can lead to disagreements about who should have authority or control over missional efforts. In addition, it can lead to a "piecemeal" approach to spirituality where Christians pick and choose their favorite service providers and outlets (as illustrated by Cynthia in chapter one), rather than understanding their relationship and responsibilities within the larger body of Christ.

But sometimes we simply operate out of *bad* models or mindsets. The four I see most frequently are a scarcity mindset, the wrong scorecards, an overemphasis on institutions, and a lack of kingdom perspective.

A scarcity mindset. "No matter the organization's size, it's easy to feel as if we don't have enough," write Peter Greer and Chris Horst. "There is always more work to do and bigger dreams to pursue."[4] In one sense, it's true that there is a limit to what people can give. For every dollar I give to one ministry, I can't give that same dollar to another. The same is true of my time and my energy, and it is certainly true that there is always more work to be done. But it can be easy to succumb to a zero-sum understanding of resources in which a dollar given to one organization is a dollar taken away from another. This is just bad theology. As Greer and Horst point out, "Too often, all we see is our little baskets instead of the One who created the fish."[5]

Wrong scorecards. Sometimes we err by using the wrong scorecards, that is, by measuring the wrong things about our ministries. For example, we may measure *inputs* such as attendance, participation, and donations received instead of *outputs* such as discipleship behaviors, missional impact, or resources shared or given away. Most of the latter are best observed in lives over time and told in stories, which do not translate well to quantitative, time-limited measurement.

Overemphasis on institutions. By this I mean that the dominant model throughout most of Christian history since Constantine has viewed institutions as the primary means of ministry. I've been in this business—and to be sure, in many ways it is a *business*—for more than thirty years. I see (and have been guilty) as much as anyone how engrained it is to focus on building our own institutions instead of unleashing Christians for missional ministry across a variety of structures or organizational "containers." It takes a lot of resources to feed the machinery we've created, sometimes to the detriment of broader kingdom ministry.

Please note that I am not dismissing institutions entirely. They can be powerful mechanisms for culture change and kingdom ministry! But today, institutions no longer engender the widespread trust they once did.[6] In addition, they can serve as anchors: great at providing stability, but a hindrance when speed and agility are needed.

Lack of kingdom perspective. The overemphasis on institutions both reflects and feeds a lack of kingdom perspective. In addition to the scarcity mindset mentioned above, an emphasis on our own empires over and above the kingdom of God leads to a mindset of control, that someone (besides God) needs to be in charge of everything.

The emphasis on leadership that has infiltrated the church in the last forty years has not helped.[7] I remember a conversation at a previous church with one of our elder board members in which he said we had to figure out how to increase our market share compared to the megachurch down the street because "the church should be run like a business."

Greer and Horst do not hesitate to call out this faulty mindset:

Deep down, we had bought the wares popular leadership gurus were selling. We baptized leadership "best practice" without testing the merits of the counsel. . . . [But] these philosophies have varying degrees of incongruence with a biblical, cruciform vision of success. . . . Our platform exists to make God's name great, not our own.[8]

Read that last sentence again. It's a subtle but most significant distinction. Yet how many times have we heard (or believed or even said) that we make God's name great *by* making our own organization great? The kingdom is not owned or facilitated by one institution.

Looking at these four erroneous mindsets, which are most easy for you to fall into?

THE RESULT

The result is what sociologists nicely call "niche overlap,"[9] illustrated in the figure below.

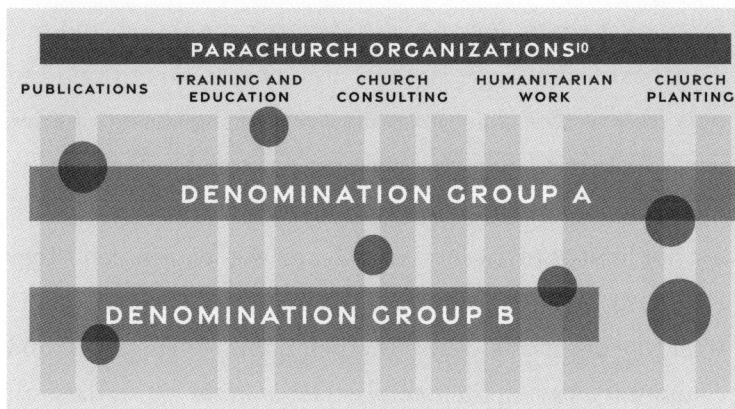

The vertical bars represent missional activities: publications, training, humanitarian work, and so on. The horizontal bars represent identity groups: Protestants generally, for example, or a denomination or network or other affiliation. The circles represent local congregations. Within each of these bars and circles are individuals. Should a Baptist who is interested in women's poverty alleviation give to their church, which contributes to the denomination's cooperative giving program to support denominational efforts in this area, or should they give directly to the denomination's agency? Should they give to a nondenominational organization or to a local entity instead?

You can see the multitude of possibilities for overlap, as the people and congregations within these shapes are going to be pulled in different directions as the organizations vie for their support. The plain name for this, although it's the one we try hardest to avoid, is *competition*: not in the sense of trying to defeat everyone else, but in vying for the same resources; for volunteers, for leaders, for time, for money, for loyalty, and for market share. Anyone who says that the church and missional extension organizations are not in competition need only look at this chart or at my overflowing basket of envelopes. They're all vying for my same resources.

But this competition and the mindsets that contribute to it are not limited to the local church and the "parachurch." They are also present between local congregations. Worship ministries take musicians away from their home congregations and community, paying them to play just another gig so they can staff their big show. Pastors recruit leaders away from other congregations. I've participated in enough local pastors' networks to observe many leaders who focus solely on their own empire and refuse to collaborate with others if it doesn't raise their own profile or improve their "bottom line" of bodies or bucks in the building.

Competition exists between missional extension organizations as well. I know of organizations in the same city, focused on ministry to the same communities or neighborhoods, with the same area of emphasis, yet with no communication or collaboration, and sometimes barely an acknowledgment of the others' existence.

I've even seen it *within* organizations. At a previous church, our pastor to young adults became upset that one of the interns he had mentored for several years within his ministry area had accepted a staff role—within the cross-cultural missions ministry of the same church!

Meanwhile, if there *is* talk of cooperation, it is often voiced as, "How do we get people to cooperate . . . with *us*?" We view ourselves at the center and others guardedly if we sense they may take from "our" resources.

We can talk about biblical legitimacy and theological differences all we want, but the actual conflict and competition lie in everyday practice. After all, "if a person begins to feel more socially connected with his parachurch men's group, then he might just decide that he will stop going to the church."[11] Then, of course, giving and literal manpower follow. Notice that "no one ever complains that the parachurch [or other ministries] is taking up prayer time that ought to be devoted to the church."[12]

Who loses by our lack of unity and cooperation? Absolutely everyone: congregations, ministry organizations, ministry leaders, individual believers . . . and last but certainly not least, the needs of the world and our witness to that watching world.

Personally, I find the opportunities and the asks overwhelming, tiring, and sometimes even guilt-inducing. My husband and I seek to be generous with our time and money. We give regularly to a variety of missional extensions, including our congregation. Yet the requests never end, and every time I get one, I feel like I am falling short in some way, neglecting an important need by saying no.

I know I'm getting pretty preachy in this chapter, but as a lifelong ministry leader, I've been guilty as well—of trying to build my own institution(s), of comparing to others, of feeling like it's too much effort to collaborate, of wanting to control. I've bought into leadership thinking that is contrary to biblical principles. All of this brought me to my a-ha moment in the classroom years ago and started me on the journey of discovery that has led to this book.

So what is the solution to these problems? I believe we need to make five difficult shifts or movements pertaining to our models and mindsets.

MOVEMENT I: FROM CONFUSION TO CLARITY

We have already examined at length the detrimental effects of a lack of understanding and clarity about the identity and nature of the church. I have suggested that we each take the time to articulate our definition and understanding of both the church and missional extensions/parachurch/para-local church/voluntary associations/charitable nonprofits, and their relationships to one another. Our practice and partnership will remain weak as long as our ecclesiology is weak or non-existent. It's time to champion the church and to instill a clear understanding of and love for the beloved body and bride of Christ in every believer, from leadership to laity.

That's the main reason I developed my doctoral elective course on "Reclaiming Ecclesiology." Every year, students tell me that it was one of the most impactful courses they have ever taken and that I should require every student to take it. So far, I have not found any other Christian colleges, seminaries, churches, or nonprofit organizations that regularly teach ecclesiology and its practical implications to their students, staff, or members. I've not heard it at any church that I've been a member of, any staff meeting at churches and nonprofits where I've served, or any school where I've studied. I'm confident this is not only my experience. Will *you* join me and elevate ecclesiology in your context?

MOVEMENT 2: FROM SCARCITY TO GENEROSITY

We have looked at why we can be prone to a scarcity mindset. The needs are great. Irrelevance, failure, and even extinction are real and constant threats, and each person's money and minutes are limited. However, while individual resources are limited, God's resources are *un*limited. What if we truly believed the long-ago statement by missionary Hudson Taylor, "God's work done in God's way will never lack God's supplies"?

A mindset of generosity is rooted in the confidence that our God is a God of abundance.

The movement from scarcity to generosity requires rooting out the sin of greed, which is best accomplished by giving away as much as you can. "Money never stays with me," John Wesley once wrote in a letter. "It would burn me if it did. I throw it out of my hands as soon as possible, lest it should find a way into my heart." What if we threw as many resources as possible *out* of our hands to the needs of the world and to other entities instead of trying to stockpile as much as possible?

Pulpit Rock Church in Colorado Springs, Colorado, has a bold goal: "We want 51 percent of everything that comes into our church to go out to other organizations," stated Rowland Smith, the Missional Culture Pastor at Pulpit Rock. The church is not there yet—currently, 33 percent of the church's income goes back out, not including the salaries of missional staff—but it is making steady progress toward spending more on the kingdom than they do on themselves.

Smith has a background serving in worship ministry and touring with rock bands. He's an experienced A/V producer and gearhead. But today, he and Pulpit Rock eschew fog machines, moving lights, and fancy production in exchange for greater impact beyond the church's walls. "There's a line we don't cross because we don't spend money on that stuff," Smith explained. "Our decisions not to do certain things allow us to join in mission and partnership with other organizations and other churches."[13]

MOVEMENT 3: FROM INSTITUTIONAL
TO MOVEMENTAL

I clearly remember a former seminary professor charting the rise and demise of institutions on a whiteboard in class:

Man———> Movement———> Monument———> Memorial

All institutions begin with a vision or a need that captures the heart of an individual or a group of people. Organization and structures are necessary to support growth and effectiveness and can help foster greater impact. But organizations and structures can become problematic if our focus becomes institutional, spending the majority of our time, effort, and resources on building up and maintaining those organizations and structures, rather than movemental, remaining agile enough to follow the leading of the Holy Spirit and remember that our institution is only one in a vast kingdom ecosystem.

Many of us have unthinkingly adopted the false assumption that organizations should live on in perpetuity. But if what if your organization is only *supposed* to exist for five, ten, or fifty years? What if you even *declared* that you would exist only for a specific time period? How would that change your mindset and your open-handedness with resources?

We have also often assumed that ministry requires a physical building to serve as "headquarters" for the work. But in the wake of the pandemic, many Christian organizations have realized that buildings can actually be a hindrance to agility. Facilities are "fixed" assets. They can cost a lot of money to maintain, especially as they age. Ministries that rent their space face ever-increasing rates. In the case of an economic downturn, fixed expenses can burden organizations beyond their financial capacity, or at least greatly restrict the resources that are available to fund their missional work. Meanwhile, many local churches use most of their space only a few days a week, meaning that the cost per hour of actual usage is even higher. While donors may be persuaded to give toward a new building project, they generally aren't enthused about giving toward rent increases, an HVAC upgrade, or paying the light bill.

As a result, many ministries are rethinking the need for central buildings or sprawling campuses. From Wycliffe Bible Translators to Lifeway to Christianity Today, some of the largest Christian ministries in the world are selling their buildings and moving to remote work and/or smaller, more flexible workspaces. For Wycliffe, the shift has meant that additional resources can go toward its work of Bible translation. "It's the strongest we've ever been in our history," said John Chesnut, Wycliffe's president and CEO. "It's just been a huge season of blessing. We're accelerating new translations, engaging or starting with new partners, faster than we ever have."[14]

MOVEMENT 4: FROM EMPIRE TO KINGDOM

"Building the Kingdom of God is a team sport, not a competition. We're better together, not apart," assert Greer and Horst.[15] What would it take—not just in theory, but in your own specific context, under your own ministry and leadership—to tear down territorialism and help build a true kingdom ecosystem? Regardless of what we say we believe, do we truly act as if we are stewards and not owners[16] of the resources entrusted to us? Scott Harris asks this hard question of leaders: "Would you go without to accomplish a Kingdom purpose?"

I confess that there are many times I would have answered no to that question. In fact, I once got very worked up that a new church plant in our city had chosen to use an almost identical name as ours. What if instead "we all periodically used 'our space' to raise awareness and funds for other nonprofits? What if we became the champions of other organizations and not just our own?"[17] What if we moved from a mindset of "a win for us is a win for the kingdom" to "a win for the kingdom is a win for us"?

The move from empire to kingdom requires ridding ourselves of the sin of envy. To start, we must stop playing the comparison game: stop asking one another how big our churches and organizations are, dropping the names of celebrities who attend or support or endorse your ministry, or reading the magazines and websites with the "largest" and "fastest growing" lists, as if any of those were *any* measure of missional effectiveness. "Nothing crushes collaboration and friendship faster than comparison."[18]

A simple way to foster a greater kingdom mindset is to install a large map in a place where those in your organization can see it regularly. On the map, use pins or markers in one color to note the needs and constituents in your context and another color to note the other ministries working in the same context: both those that have different missions but within the same location (such as a church, a foster agency, and a teen ministry in the same community) and the same mission but based in different locations (such as different missionary agencies focused on the same continent, country, or people group). At least once a week, spend time praying for the people and ministry efforts represented by the marks on the map, thanking the Lord for their work and asking for their blessing. Once a month, meet in-person or virtually with a leader from one of the other ministries, getting to know what they do, celebrating their successes, and learning how you can support and encourage them.

MOVEMENT 5: FROM CONTROL TO FREEDOM

Most who write about the relationship between the church and missional extensions note that disagreements, even those couched as theological in nature, are ultimately about authority, power, and control. As Scheitle wryly points out, "The problem is not with free enterprise but with enterprise that challenges the territory of the current powers."[19]

We would do well to remember once again that we are only stewards, not owners. They're not "our people" and it's not "our money." In addition, the church was established by Jesus, who sent the Holy Spirit to empower and guide us. Do we seek that guidance, and do we truly trust the Spirit, not just to direct us but direct others? In all my years as a member of a local congregation, I can probably count on one hand the number of times I've heard a leader say of an opportunity or an ask, "Pray about it, discern the Spirit, and give (or serve) where the Lord directs." What if we gave that kind of freedom to everyone within our sphere of leadership, teaching them first how to hear and discern the voice of the Spirit, and then encouraging them to obey that voice? Doing so would require us to relinquish our sense of control, and when we get right down to it, most of us don't really want to submit to someone else's authority.

I have always been intrigued by the story of Paul and Barnabas and their "sharp disagreement" over whether to bring John Mark with them on their missionary journey (Acts 15:36-41). Weren't they both led by the Spirit? If so, then how did they come to such different conclusions? Are we willing to relinquish control so that the Spirit can lead freely, even when it causes sharp disagreements? The reality is that the people and the work of the Spirit are blown like the wind, not controlled by any individual or organization (John 3:8). Will we release those people and that work to full freedom in the Spirit?

Mikey Lynch, a ministry leader in Australia and author of *The Vine Movement*, has observed that Christian organizations in his country *have* to cooperate because of Australia's relatively small population (twenty-six million) spread over a large geographic area, compounded by a steady decline in Christian belief that initially outpaced the United States by several decades. In 1976 the number of Australians who identified as Christian dipped below 80 percent for the first time. By 2021 that number had declined to 43.9 percent, with only 2 percent of Australians reporting regular church attendance.

"It forces collaboration," said Lynch, who reports a "broad but variegated" ecumenist spirit among Christians in the country. To some extent in Australia, "a Christian is a Christian is a Christian" even though the landscape is dominated by denominations that are hierarchical rather than associational in structure, including Catholics, Anglicans, Uniting Church, and Presbyterians.

While America tends toward a free-market, competitive economy of Christian ministry, many Australian Christians have leaned in to work together. Some of the collaborations have been "forced" or born of necessity, such as when one ministry can't afford a building while another has extra space in theirs. Other partnerships are "principled," based on shared goals and values. Another effective arrangement is cross-staffing, where separate organizations join together to pay the full-time salary for a staff person who splits time working for both ministries, inherently fostering greater communication and collaboration.[20]

But more than making these five movements, we need an entirely new framework or *paradigm* to guide our thinking, our language, and our actions regarding these shifts. In the next chapter I'll flesh out this new paradigm and introduce you to examples of what this new paradigm might look like in action.

9

HOW CAN WE
WORK TOGETHER?

A NEW PARADIGM FOR THE NEXT CENTURY

So, we have finally come to the big question and the central aim of this book: How can we work together, truly becoming the whole church for the whole world for the twenty-first century?

THE OLD MODEL: A COLLECTION OF CYLINDERS

I believe we need to move from an institutional perspective of the church and the "parachurch" to a *functional* perspective, restoring as central the apostolic nature of the body of Christ—all believers, not just those who feel called to "vocational" ministry—for kingdom ministry as part of the *missio Dei*.

The current and historic structural perspective can be imagined as a group of cylinders as seen in the figure below.

Each container represents a local church or a nonprofit organization. Some are bigger, some are smaller. Some have a wider footprint, others have a narrow reach and focus. The height of each cylinder represents how protective the entity and its

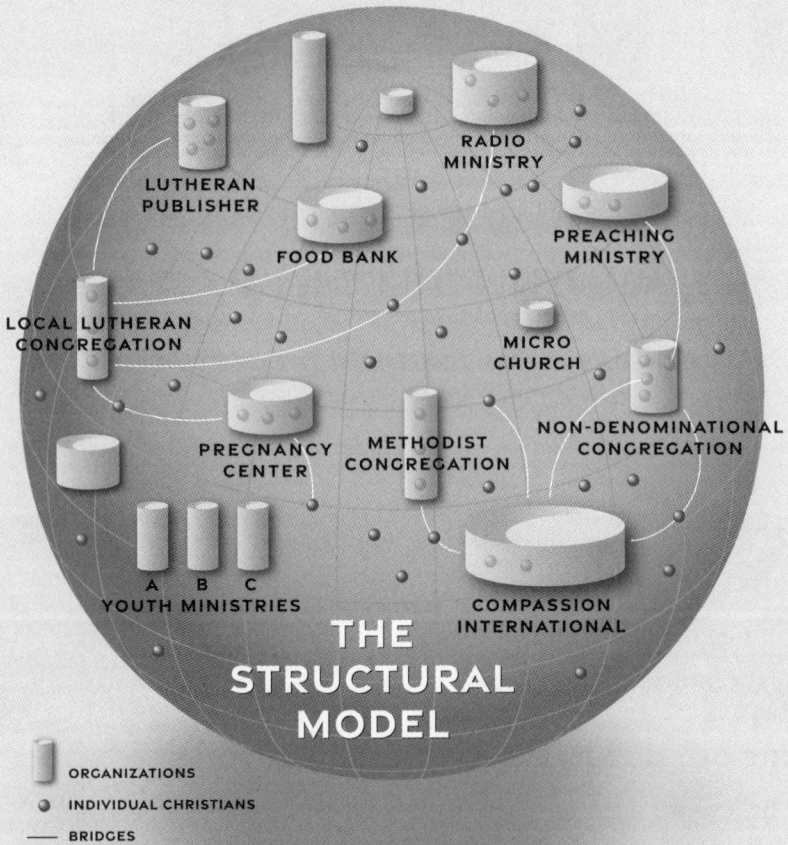

THE
STRUCTURAL
MODEL

LUTHERAN
PUBLISHER

RADIO
MINISTRY

FOOD BANK

PREACHING
MINISTRY

LOCAL LUTHERAN
CONGREGATION

MICRO
CHURCH

PREGNANCY
CENTER

METHODIST
CONGREGATION

NON-DENOMINATIONAL
CONGREGATION

A   B   C
YOUTH MINISTRIES

COMPASSION
INTERNATIONAL

ORGANIZATIONS
INDIVIDUAL CHRISTIANS
BRIDGES

leaders are of its "walls" in relationship to the other entities, and of the people within it. The walls are generally theological in nature, indicating who is "in" and who is "out" based on beliefs not just about essentials of the faith, but about the nature and role of that entity. For example, a "local church only" perspective of ministry would result in very high walls, reflecting the belief that everything should happen within and from that cylinder.

Some cylinders have walkways or bridges between them. These are created by mutual agreement based on some sense of affinity, whether beliefs, mission and goals, methods, or location. In this graphic, a local Lutheran congregation has bridges to a local pregnancy center and to denominational entities.

You'll notice that nonprofit organizations generally have lower walls. As we've explored earlier, many Christian nonprofit organizations are non- or interdenominational in nature, welcoming participation by individuals from a variety of theological streams.

Within and between these cylinders are individuals, represented in the graphic by the dots. There are individuals who clearly reside within one cylinder, and some of them may cross bridges or go out from time to time. But there are many others in the land between the cylinders. Some, like Cynthia in chapter one, have some sort of relationship with multiple cylinders, whether for service, for pure consumption, or a combination of both. Many of these individuals are not grounded or rooted anywhere; they just wander from cylinder to cylinder, as the leaders of those cylinders call to them: "Join us! Stay here! We're doing it better!"

In recognition of the reality of niche overlap, you can also see that an individual who identifies as a member of a particular local congregation but who wants to support those in need could either stay within their cylinder, walk the bridge to the partner organization, or step *out* of the cylinder to be involved with one of the other cylinders. Meanwhile, whether raised intentionally or not, the height of the walls can reflect an organization's sense of "ownership" of the people within their cylinder.

There is another name for these cylinders. They are called silos, and I believe they have a crippling effect on the worldwide work of the gospel. We spend so much time and money building and maintaining our silos that we become disconnected from the greater kingdom picture.

Hear me well: I am *not* anti-organization or anti-institution. My doctoral studies and much of my teaching and writing have focused on organizational leadership of churches and Christian ministries. I recognize that there is great power and potential in organizing people to accomplish a goal they could not reach on their own. However, there is also great danger in institutionalism, in believing that institutions and organizations themselves are the center, the source, even the goal, instead of simply the *means* for equipping and unleashing the body of Christ.

The fulfillment of God's mission on earth is accomplished through *people*, not through institutions. This is counter to the way many of us have been conditioned through decades, even centuries, of education and practice. Sure, we know that institutions are made up of people, but we tend to have an institution-first or institution-central view: we start the organization, then look for people to join it and support it. That may have been effective in a different time, but today this perspective can get in the way of fulfilling our mission to a world in need. Plus, I think it reflects a modern cultural understanding more than the true biblical nature of the church as the apostolic people of God.

Instead of this institutional view, let's look at what a functional perspective might look like.

THE NEW MODEL: MISSIONAL EXTENSIONS

Again, I suggest that instead of church or "parachurch," we pivot to a paradigm of *missional extensions*.

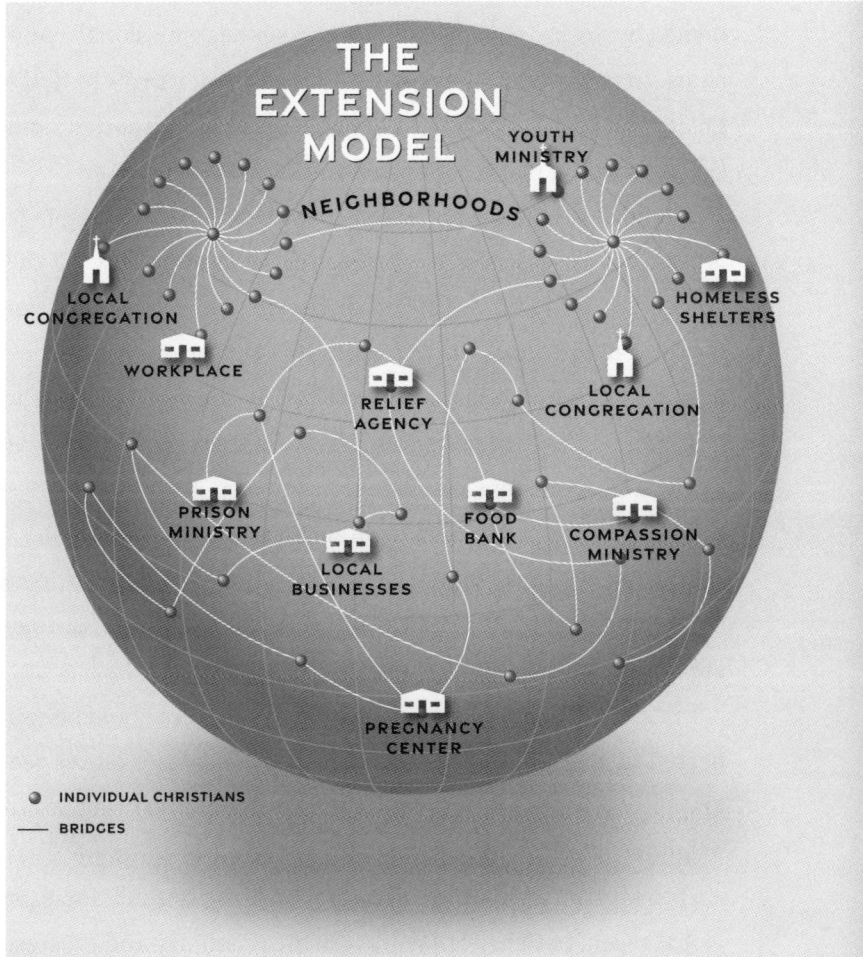

Instead of vertical cylinders or silos, this paradigm takes a flatter, horizontal view. Imagine nodes on a network that covers the globe: a map of a world of missional extensions, in which the smallest unit is the individual believer, but it is not the *only* unit. Missional extensions can and should consist of individual believers, local congregations, local nonprofits, and organizations whose work reaches to the edges of the earth. Even Christian-owned businesses in any industry can serve as missional extensions. In this model (1) every entity is aware of its role in God's greater mission; (2) every entity is connected to another; and (3) every individual is connected to a local congregation.

I believe the missional extensions paradigm and language is much more faithful to the biblical understanding of the mission of God and the role that the church as the people of God is called to play in that mission. The term *missional* reminds us of our ultimate purpose, while the word *extensions* reminds us that wherever we are, we are representatives of Christ and agents of God's mission. The responsibility belongs to us, not to an institution or some type of corporate shell.

In this paradigm, organizations are simply containers, conduits which facilitate the flow of every-believer mission; they are not the center or the focus. The local church is the starting point: not for control, but because every believer should be connected to an *ekklēsia*. The local church is also at the center geographically, in terms of its reach. The local church is best at near-neighbor missionality, at meeting needs close to home. That isn't to say that local churches cannot have regional, national, or global reach, but they enjoy the closest proximity and greatest opportunity to meet the needs immediately surrounding them.

In addition, the *ekklēsia* provides something that other non-profit organizations mostly cannot: the opportunity to be formed in community, through regular participation in shared worship and everyday relationship. This, too, is part of God's mission, to reconcile all things to one another and to himself. From there, we join God's work wherever he has called and placed us.

Meanwhile, there are a multitude of other missional extension organizations, historically known as parachurch organizations, which mobilize believers to do the work of the kingdom in a focused area, whether that is a particular purpose, a geographic location, or some other delineator. And individuals, as missional extensions themselves, can join God's work via a number of conduits. Some may focus on their neighborhood or their workplace. Others may have a heart for their city, while still others may feel called to go to the farthest reaches of the earth.

Note that in this paradigm, we must view the whole world as "flat"—not in terms of geological shape, but as an even playing field for kingdom ministry, in which believers around the globe are impacting their own Jerusalem, Judea, and Samaria, and *their* ends of the earth. The West is no longer the center or the seat of power of Christianity, and we must let go of traditional geographic and colonial borders and hierarchies. What is "local" to us may be someone else's ends of the earth. No individual or single institution or entity owns any particular territory, anywhere in the world.

Another advantage of the missional extensions paradigm is that it fosters unity among the entire body of Christ. As Eugene Kim has said, we have "dismembered" the body of Christ into divisions: between church and parachurch, between denominations, even between segregated ministries within the local congregation.[1] By viewing every one of us as missional extensions, we recognize our shared mission even though we each have different roles to play. And while the missional extension paradigm doesn't immediately eliminate the problem of niche overlap, it at least has the potential for freer flow between containers.

A NEW FLOW FOR KINGDOM FUNDING

Along with reframing the way we view individuals and organizations, a missional extension paradigm also leads us to rethink our dominant financial models. In the current institutional or cylinder framework, each entity tries to collect as many material resources as possible. The majority of those resources stay within that entity, while some may be distributed elsewhere.

That's okay . . . to a point. The problem is that most of the time, the *majority* of resources are not going to those with the greatest need. Instead, those of us in Western contexts, and particularly within the United States, are governed by a capitalist, entitlement mindset instead of by a generosity mindset: what's mine is yours, because you need it more.

A few years ago, I was appalled and deeply convicted to learn from a class presentation by an international student that many American churches put the majority of their large budgets toward the Sunday-morning worship gathering— while around the world, many believers do not have access to Scripture, reliable sources of food, or even drinking water. Folks, this is just plain wrong.

In addition, I see church networks and denominations and some Christian ministries who are more interested in franchising their brand into new territory than in supporting the indigenous work in those areas, whether those are across town or across the world. Church planters have often been coached to focus on areas with the greatest "growth potential," generally meaning population and income growth, rather than areas in decline and with the greatest spiritual and material needs. Because, let's be honest, a church in an impoverished area takes more resources than it gives, and we like seeing our names on the lists of biggest and fastest-growing churches.

Is this socialism? Nope, it's a kingdom mindset. Let's revisit the early church as described in Acts: the believers had everything in common, sold property and possessions to give to anyone who had need, and took up collections to send with the apostles to other congregations. It's time we ask ourselves some hard questions about how we are stewarding all of the resources we have been given and to think, once again, in terms of the overall kingdom and missional extensions instead of centralized institutions.

What if, instead of focusing on starting a congregation, a church planter started a Christian nonprofit in a community, and a faith community emerged out of that? What if we decided to do away with the full-time professional, salaried model that has dominated the Western church for the last century? What if we focused on giving away more than we kept, even if that is to our own perceived detriment? Shifting our paradigm from an institutional model to one of missional extensions will force us to wrestle with these and other hard questions as we seek to live out of a completely new understanding.

FROM PARADIGM TO PRACTICE

What might real-life ministry based on a paradigm of missional extensions look like? What follows are examples of different efforts to bridge the historical divides. None of them use the term "missional extensions" (yet!), but they all reflect a desire to rethink and re-invent traditional models. They are stories from a variety of contexts; as you read through them, keep in mind that there is no one "right" way, and there are many other models and examples that leaders around the world are experimenting with. The purpose here is to broaden your horizons and to spur your own imagination.

Moving toward a missional culture: Pulpit Rock Church. In addition to the goal of directing more than half of all gifts received to other ministries, Pulpit Rock Church in Colorado has been working to install a missional *culture* throughout the organization, moving from a "come-to-us," inward-focused church to an outward-looking congregation. Rowland Smith, Missional Culture Pastor, has led a multi-pronged approach toward achieving the church's goal.

One component, of course, is providing outlets and opportunities for congregational giving and service. A first step toward that end was to change the focus of the church's annual Christmas offering, directing all receipts toward needs in the community instead of the church's yearly budget. The first Christmas offering brought in between $10,000 and $15,000. Most recently, Pulpit Rock gathered $180,000, which was distributed to a handful of causes and organizations in the community.

During the rest of the year, church staff members engage with members of the congregation and the broader community, listening to what they are involved in and looking for ways to get involved. "There is a top-down element, but we have also funded a lot of things via the ground up or relationally," Smith said. "We're getting better at asking, 'What is God up to? Let's join that,' as opposed to 'Here's a cool idea.'"

But beyond logistics, Smith and his colleagues have worked to embed a missional mindset into the entire congregation, helping every member view themselves as missional practitioners. "It's great to come up with X, Y, and Z about how we're going to do this, but there's a culture-making piece that happens over time," said Smith. "What has also shifted along with the practice of joining God in mission is the way that we talk theologically from the stage. We talk more about kingdom than about getting saved."

As part of Pulpit Rock's connection process for new folks, various staff members teach about the ethos of the church, including an entire session by Smith on the concept of the kingdom of God and on kingdom language. "A lot of them are Christians and have heard of the kingdom. They know it's in the Bible," Smith said, "but they haven't heard of it as a driving thing. It's a paradigm shift." Pulpit Rock has also experimented with a "Living Sent" cohort experience that includes both classroom time and praxis opportunities in downtown Colorado Springs. "We're still experimenting with 'discipleship from the pew to the pavement,'" Smith acknowledged.

In addition, the church staff makes strategic and programming decisions based on the foundational value of kingdom mission. These discussions focus just as much on what *won't* get time and money as much as on what will. "We make decisions on what we're not going to do because what you decide not to do impacts your missional posture," Smith said. In addition, Smith firmly believes that every decision disciples a congregation in a particular direction. He and the staff at Pulpit Rock are always asking what their decisions are discipling people toward.

But to Smith, the most important factor toward culture shift is storytelling. "People respond to stories more than they do an institutional effort." He pointed to the nonprofit Charity: Water as an example. "Instead of saying, 'Give to Charity: Water and we'll travel around the world helping to improve water supply,' they say, 'You can give so much per month and give this village clean water for this specific amount of time,'" Smith said. "That's a tangible result. We try to show people the tangible result" through videos and personal stories shared online, on-stage, and in-person.[2]

Catalyzing ministry at unreached colleges: EveryCampus. The rise of parachurch organizations in the twentieth century included the birth of dozens of organizations focused specifically on ministry to college campuses. Some of those are now nationally or even internationally known, while others focus on a specific school or region of the country. They include both denominational and nondenominational organizations.

In 2017, two of the largest of these ministries, InterVarsity Christian Fellowship and Cru (formerly Campus Crusade for Christ), began to formally work together and reach out to other campus ministries to form a coalition. The resulting entity, EveryCampus, now includes more than one hundred partner organizations, including denominations and local churches.

Their focus is on the nearly eighteen hundred college campuses around the United States that do not yet have a known, organized gospel presence.

"God took the goodwill, trust, and relationships that had been built and we said, 'We can do better than just kind of being nice to each other,'" said Jon Hietbrink of InterVarsity Christian Fellowship. "The driving question was, 'What could we do together that we could never do on our own?'"[3]

EveryCampus uses its digital platform to provide partner ministries and potential leaders with resources to help launch gospel communities on unreached campuses. One of these resources is a map of all collegiate ministries across the country, the first of its kind. This map has helped partners see regional and national patterns, areas of duplicate ministry, as well as schools with no outreach efforts. The latter group consists mostly of smaller schools including community colleges, historically black colleges and universities (HBCUs), and institutions that primarily serve Hispanic communities.

Besides their shared commitment to reaching college students, EveryCampus partners agree to the Lausanne Covenant, a doctrinal statement created in 1974 under the leadership of John Stott in cooperation with the representatives of the more than 150 nations that gathered for the very first International Congress on World Evangelization in Lausanne, Switzerland.[4] Both EveryCampus and Lausanne serve as neutral conveners and catalysts for like-minded ministry leaders, helping them see each other as collaborators, not competitors.

Rethinking church economics: Mosaic Church. Mark DeYmaz, founding pastor of Mosaic Church in Little Rock,

Arkansas, is a natural entrepreneur and outside-the-box thinker. When he saw trends in charitable giving pointing to a long decline, DeYmaz began to rethink the traditional approach of churches relying on tithes and offerings to fund their activities.

"A church's need for money never goes away, and the pressure for more of it that senior leaders feel and live with is a constant," DeYmaz wrote in *The Coming Revolution in Church Economics: Why Tithes and Offerings Are No Longer Enough.*[5] Experiencing this pressure in their own church, DeYmaz and Senior Pastor Harry Li started looking for ways to generate more income rather than simply hoping for increased giving.

The solution at Mosaic Church has been what DeYmaz calls the "church-based nonprofit." In 2008, Mosaic started Vine and Village, a separate 501(c)3 nonprofit organization that is headquartered at Mosaic. Vine and Village operates on four strategic tiers. At the top level are what DeYmaz calls their "signature programs"—programs so intrinsic to the church's identity that they are near-permanent ministries of Vine and Village. These include a chess club, a ministry to those with disabilities, a food distribution program, and an assistance ministry to low-income people in the community.

The second tier consists of short-term programs that have a predetermined shelf life. For example, for five years Vine and Village ran an AAU basketball team for kids ages 8-12. The third tier is for incubating new ministries: at the time of this writing, Vine and Village was getting ready to move a ministry to immigrants out of the church building and into a local medical clinic. The fourth tier consists of partnerships with dozens of other local, state, and federal entities: Vine and Village rents office space to external nonprofits and shares other resources for the good of the community.

While there is overlap in leadership of the two organizations— for example, a staff member of Vine and Village might also serve as an elder at Mosaic—the two entities are structurally separate. "The metaphor we use is that they are two sisters who live in the same house," DeYmaz said of Mosaic and Vine and Village. "Vine and Village is a separate legal nonprofit but most people wouldn't be able to differentiate between the two. It's just another aspect of the church. You can volunteer in the children's ministry, in the chess club, in the food bank, or in the ESL classes. It's all part of the family."

At the same time, as a separate nonprofit, Vine and Village is eligible for grant funding that would not be available to Mosaic Church. In addition, people in the community are more inclined to be involved in the ministries of a nonprofit than to attend a church. Vine and Village partners with other nonprofits to benefit the local community, and other churches in Little Rock will send financial support and volunteers to assist the ministries of Vine and Village. "If those ministries were done by Mosaic Church, it's possible those things might happen, but generally it's a safe assumption that if something is done under the auspices of a church, other churches are reticent to send people or money," DeYmaz said.[6]

Shortly after my conversation with DeYmaz, he texted me several photos from activities in Mosaic's building that morning that showed the overlap of activities between Mosaic Church, Vine and Village, and other community organizations. Through these activities and partnerships, Vine and Village brings significant income to Mosaic Church while also making a significant impact in the community. Mosaic Church is a central institution where people come to worship, and Vine and Village enables it to extend branches throughout the Little Rock area.

A community-wide ecosystem: Church United. The news in the South Florida Christian community was not good: in short succession, six local pastors had succumbed to moral failure, two of those in high-profile churches. What was going on? Eddie Copeland and his colleagues at the National Christian Foundation (NCF) in South Florida decided to gather a group of pastors to find out.

"We brought fourteen senior pastors into a room at a restaurant," recalled Copeland, "and we quickly discovered there was something wrong in the soil. They viewed each other as competition. They weren't feeling supported." In an area of the country that was rapidly becoming post-Christian, NCF South Florida began to ask what a thirty-year view of community transformation would look like. "If we all believe the church (as the people of God) is God's 'Plan A' for renewal, we're going to have to work with our churches and bring ministries and nonprofits together," Copeland explained.

As a result of that meeting, NCF South Florida committed to a deep investment in the health and wholeness of the local churches in the area under the philosophy that healthy leaders lead to thriving churches, which lead to a flourishing city. They approached potential donors and asked if they would consider giving to a soul care fund for church and ministry leaders. The response was overwhelming, with $1 million invested over three years. "We became the trusted third party between investors and the local church, and a safe third space between pastors and ministry leaders," said Copeland.

The response by pastors and ministry leaders was equally positive—and instructive. "You guys have my back, and I've never experienced this," pastors told Copeland and his colleagues. "You wanted nothing from me; instead, you wanted something *for* me." The soul care initiative bought incredible trust with pastors and ministry leaders in the area. In turn, they started inviting NCF to talk to *their* givers, and NCF began to mobilize Christians from across congregations to meet the greatest needs in the community.

These efforts eventually birthed an entity called Church United, one of three initiatives of the South Florida branch of the National Christian Foundation, the largest Christian grant maker in the world. As a philanthropic catalyst, NCF helps Christians steward their resources through a variety of charitable giving avenues such as Donor Advised Funds (DAFs). But local branches of NCF can also develop their own initiatives and strategies. So, in addition to working with the local donor community, NCF South Florida began to connect with the business community and to bring area churches and ministries together.

"We're building an ecosystem," Copeland said. "It's like an orchestra. Everyone is playing in the key of C but we are bringing the trumpets, flutes, and trombones together." Everyone views each other's work as equal, a part of *the* church. In 2018, a nineteen-year-old opened fire on students and staff at Marjory Stoneman Douglas High School in a Miami suburb, killing seventeen people and injuring seventeen others. In the aftermath of the nightmare, Church United mobilized ministries and donors to provide counseling for students, pay medical bills for victims, and re-do the exterior of the entire school building to help erase the memory of that horrible event.

"We were able to say, 'Your bill was paid for by the people of God in South Florida because we don't want this to be the story of South Florida that you remember,'" Copeland recalled. Church United has also helped organize hurricane response and relief efforts in addition to a wide variety of mercy and justice initiatives that serve Dade, Broward, and Palm Beach Counties. Brought together in partnership, donors, individual believers, local congregations, the business community, and ministry leaders all feel they are part of bringing change and transformation to South Florida.

Every member on mission: Brentwood Baptist Church. When someone is interested in becoming a member at Brentwood Baptist Church in Brentwood, Tennessee, they engage in a new members' sequence that helps them understand what the church is all about. One of the key pieces of the church's DNA is getting every single member serving, whether that is inside or outside the church.

"We have a high expectation membership here," explained Michele Dyer, the Member Development Minister at Brentwood Baptist. "At the membership meetings, we explain that our church is here to serve and support you in whatever way possible, but we also believe that God has called you to ministry. Our job as staff is to equip the saints for the work of the ministry; we're not here to do all the ministry ourselves."

That process involves helping members identify their gifts, passions, and sense of calling, and then suggesting matching opportunities within the church or with a number of partner ministries in the local community and beyond. "Our philosophy [at Brentwood Baptist] is that it's impossible for our church to do all the types of ministries that need to be out there to meet the needs of the community, so why not partner with them, so why not send them the servants that they need?" Dyer said.

This philosophy was embedded in the church over the forty-year tenure of its recently retired senior pastor, Mike Glenn, and is now deeply rooted throughout the church's leadership and across its nine campuses. "Everyone functions under that premise as we talk to people about engagement and service—this idea that we need to engage people in their calling and their passion rather than trying to fill holes in things that we need done within the church," Dyer said. "This means that in our approach we have to be really open-handed. It may mean that someone never serves on Sunday morning because they've been serving elsewhere two to three times a week." This open-handedness can also be seen in the fact that the church doesn't control or formally approve external opportunities.

"The partner ministries are just a suggestion and known relationships," Dyer explained. "We encourage them to find places that are the right fit. Our pastor often quips that if they have a passion and gifting for ministering to left-handed truck drivers, we want to support them in finding that type of ministry. Just because we don't know about a particular ministry doesn't inhibit us from helping them get connected."

While Brentwood Baptist Church has over 10,000 members and sees weekly attendance of 6,000–7,000 between its campuses, Dyer firmly believes that effective member mobilization does not depend on church size. The critical components for any church include (1) senior leadership that is completely committed to the idea of engaging people in their calling; (2) recognition that the equipping and mobilizing process is a marathon, not a sprint. It must be a long-term commitment by the entire organization, not a temporary initiative; and (3) having someone, whether a staff person or a high-capacity volunteer, who is committed to serving as a champion and leader of the ministry. In addition, Brentwood Baptist utilizes trained lay coaches who meet with new members and help them determine opportunities for them to engage in their areas of giftedness, calling, and passion.

Dyer clearly has found a place for hers as she champions this type of ministry to other churches. "I see a movement happening in the church, and not just in a specific denomination," she said. "We're starting to see more of an open-handedness with pastors who recognize there is so much benefit in just getting people engaged in what they're passionate about. For decades the church has been so internally focused. We've told people that discipleship is all about coming to a class. But that's not the end of the process. We need to begin to turn outward toward someone else."

OTHER CREATIVE IDEAS

In addition to the more detailed cases described above, here are some other ideas to consider:

- A church in Colorado encourages its congregants to practice what they call "5+5 Giving." Based on the concept of a tithe, the church encourages their people to give

5 percent to the church and 5 percent to missionaries, mission teams, or strategic partners.

- The Christian musician Michael Card routinely submitted lyrics for his songs to his pastor for theological accountability and approval.

- City Gospel Movements, birthed out of the Luis Palau Association and Tim Keller's Redeemer City to City, have been rapidly growing around the world. These movements seek to unite the citywide church, develop leaders, and strengthen gospel witness in their cities.

- A church in central Texas encourages its small groups to serve together in local ministries.

- A congregation developed a goal of having each member give 1 percent to a ministry partner in the form of one day of service per quarter, five minutes a day in prayer, and one dollar out of one hundred dollars in income.

- Many churches provide opportunities for parachurch ministries to recruit volunteers from the congregation. These partners are mentioned regularly from the platform. Some churches hold an annual "ministry fair" to make congregants aware of opportunities to serve.

- A pastor I know reduced his hours to part-time with an accompanying pay cut so that more of the church's funds could be directed to needs in the community.

- Mission Increase, a kingdom bridge-building organization, encourages nonprofit ministries to thank the leaders at each of the churches where their volunteers attend. "Partnership is a *person*," noted Scott Harris, Vice

President of Church and Global Engagement at Mission Increase. "We had nonprofit leaders write letters to the pastors: 'Did you know that [name of congregant] does these things for us? Thank you for equipping her and for gifting her to us.'"

■ Some churches and nonprofits have taken a "parish" approach, assuming shared responsibility for the spiritual and material needs in a particular limited geographic area.

■ A church in a small city in the UK operates a cafe in a historic building in the town square. In addition to serving the community as a typical coffee shop, patrons subsidize meals for visitors in need. The building also has meeting spaces that are utilized by a variety of community groups and organizations, making it a center of the community both geographically and functionally.

What ideas might God be stirring in you for your specific ministry context?

THE FRONTIER: RETHINKING
RELIGIOUS INFRASTRUCTURE

The examples above are based on what is largely seen and known, but there are also methodological frontiers that are yet to be explored, and which some of us may not be able to invent or even imagine from our current vantage point. In her provocative article "The Spiritual Infrastructure of the Future," Sue Phillips, co-founder of Sacred Design Lab, notes the growing gap between traditional stewards of religious assets, such as denominations and other formal organizations, and the needs of contemporary religious seekers and communities. The long-standing infrastructure—the combination of mechanisms meant to "create, collect, distribute and control resources"—no longer works in many contexts.

The same is true in the church-parachurch world. As we move into a world that is increasingly non-ecclesial, post-denominational, and exvangelical, we need spiritual innovators to create new infrastructures—new ways of participating in kingdom work and enabling flow within and between missional extensions. Phillips borrows the concept of "desire paths" from landscape architecture: it's the idea that you don't install sidewalks to direct where people should walk; you add them after you see where people *actually* walk. Who knows what some of us might discover or create if we ask the Lord to give us eyes to see new opportunities and potential pathways![7]

10

WHERE DO WE GO
FROM HERE?

PRACTICAL SUGGESTIONS FOR LEADERS
AND LAYPEOPLE

Thank you for journeying with me through this book. My hope is that you have been both challenged and encouraged as you have considered the redemptive impact that a fully functioning, missionally extended, *whole* church might have on the world. As we prepare to part ways, I'd like to suggest four steps we all must take to reshape our conversation and our practice for faithful ministry in this new world.

REPENT

I believe our first step must be to humble our hearts and *repent* of the many erroneous beliefs and practices that have contributed to the loss of trust and lack of unity that we are experiencing today. You can use the litany that follows as a starting point for reflection and confession not only individually, but also corporately in staff and leadership teams and in congregations and other groups. I encourage you to take your time reading through, reflecting on, and responding to each of them.

For having a low, negative, or dismissive view of the church, the beautiful bride of Christ:

Lord, we humbly repent.

For a spirit of jealousy toward our brothers and sisters and their ministries:

Lord, we humbly repent.

For a scarcity mindset in our organizations and in our personal lives:

Lord, we humbly repent.

For thinking that it is our job to make Jesus famous and that this happens best by making ourselves and our organizations famous:

Lord, we humbly repent.

For a spirit of competition that has led us to compare to others instead of to your calling:

Lord, we humbly repent.

For the times we have equated organizational growth with your favor when they are not necessarily the same:

Lord, we humbly repent.

For our arrogance any time we have thought or acted as though we, and not God, have done the work or brought growth:

Lord, we humbly repent.

For equating nonprofit Christian organizations and gatherings with the *ekklēsia*:

Lord, we humbly repent.

For the church not being the church to one another and to the world and thereby tarnishing our witness:

Lord, we humbly repent.

For thinking of the church—in any form—as a business or no different from any other earthly organization, and for uncritically adopting worldly principles in our leadership and management:

Lord, we humbly repent.

For not pursuing and prioritizing the unity that Jesus prayed for so earnestly:

Lord, we humbly repent.

For territorialism, for thinking in terms of *our* turf and *our* people instead of realizing that all are temporary gifts from God for us to steward:

Lord, we humbly repent.

For the times that we have thought that *our* way—our doctrine, our methods—is the only right way:

Lord, we humbly repent.

For hoarding resources within our organizations instead of directing them to the areas of greatest spiritual and material need in our communities and around the world:

Lord, we humbly repent.

For believing that our country or region of the world is more special to you and that others should be like us:

Lord, we humbly repent.

Take some time to listen to the Holy Spirit for other areas in which you may need to repent or lament. What is the Lord saying to you as you make space to humbly listen?

RECLAIM

Once we have taken appropriate time to reflect, repent, and re-offer ourselves humbly to God, we need to *reclaim* the true nature, purpose, and power of the church, in all its history and mystery and unique forms. In other words, we need to revisit our ecclesiology—or perhaps, for many of us, consider it for the first time.

One aspect of this involves reclaiming the apostolic (missional) nature of the church. However, we must also reclaim the nature of the church as a sacramental, participatory community, the *gathered* people of God, the *ekklēsia*. Part of loving the church includes loving and participating in the local church, despite its many warts and flaws. Individual believers should gather regularly. The idea of a Christian who does not belong to a congregation would have been unheard of throughout most of history and unthinkable to the apostles and the early church Fathers.

Loving the Lord in corporate worship, loving one another in community, and loving our neighbors in mission are both the primary ways we are formed in the ways of Christ and our primary witness to the power of the gospel. Believers can't belong only to the "invisible," global church without any connection to the "visible," gathered church. I know there have been all sorts of abuses perpetrated by church leaders, and many of us have been terribly wounded by leaders claiming the authority of Christ in denominations, networks, and congregations. Still, that does not mean that God's intention or priority for the church has changed.

Years ago, when NASA was figuring out how to feed astronauts on space missions, there was talk of the possibility that one day humans would be able to get the majority of their nutrients via food pills. Scientists had determined the exact nutrients the human body needed, and these could be extracted from food or produced in a laboratory and then distilled and manufactured in the form of pills. Those who consumed them could lose weight by eliminating taste and smell, which stimulated hunger and contributed to overeating.

But science and our own experience have told us that the body needs more than just a collection of individual nutrients. Take, for example, the act of eating an apple. We need the sensory experiences of seeing, smelling, and tasting our food, not to mention the entire process of digestion. That first sweet smell. The rumble in our stomach, signaling our hunger. The feel of the apple in our hand as we bring it to our lips. The sensation of our teeth breaking the skin, then chewing the flesh. The flavor of the juice on our taste buds, and the feeling as some of it dribbles out of our mouth and down our chin. These processes impact not only the proper functioning of our digestive system from start to (ahem) finish, but also our emotional health. We derive joy from the smell, the taste, the touch, the anticipation, the satisfaction.

Friends, I know too many people who think of church as no different from a food pill. We can each create our own spiritual nutritional formula consisting of some combination of Bible study, prayer, fellowship, worship, service, and perhaps sacraments, consuming them via a collection of individual "pills" from different sources: a small group here, a worship experience there, a service project elsewhere.

But the church is not merely a collection of nutrients; *it is an apple*. We benefit, and we benefit others, by our shared participation in a community that is unlike anything this world knows or can provide. We receive nutrients from corporate worship, from re-centering around the work of the cross, from rubbing shoulders as we serve together, from the messy work of learning to live with and love people who are not like us. There is simply no biblical, theological, or formational substitute for regular, committed participation in a community of believers.

There are many times I have wished that what I just wrote were not true. Living the Christian life by myself is easier—certainly more convenient and less messy—but it is not possible. As Edward Klink III wrote, "The very idea that a person could be a Christian without going to church is to misunderstand both 'Christian' and 'church.' It is an implicit denial of connection to Christ to avoid expressed commitment and connection to a gathering local body."[1]

Lest you think I am coming from a position of strident legalism, let me assure you that I am *not* saying that a Christian should be part of an institution at all costs. There are times when it is absolutely necessary to leave a particular *ekklēsia*, or to take a break because of the need for healing from significant and deep wounds. As I write this, I am gingerly stepping back into participation in local congregational life after an extended season of rest and recovery following decades of ministry leadership and life as a pastor's wife, with all the joys and pains that attend those roles.

At the same time, the realities of significant hurt and abuse do not negate the importance of the body of Christ in God's plan for the world, and for our own formation in the ways of Jesus. Therefore, while some of us are taking a break and others are tending to those who are wounded, let the rest of us put all of our strength toward reimagining, reforming, and rebuilding the church to the glory of his name.

In addition, as part of reclaiming the nature and purpose of the church (our ecclesiology), we must also reclaim *our* identity as the church, the body of Christ. Reclaiming the sentness and apostolic nature of the church means also reclaiming our sentness as believers. Each of us bears responsibility for taking the whole gospel to the whole world; it is not something we can abdicate to leaders or clergy or institutions. It also means reclaiming our belonging and contributions to a corporate body, not just participation as attendees or consumers or individuals. Remember, the church is *us*, not an abstract concept, a building, a corporate entity, or any of the other many ways we divorce the church from our identity as followers of Christ. May we all reclaim a vision and love for the church, and a clear understanding of our relationship, role, and responsibilities to it.

REFRAME

Upon reclaiming our vision for the church, we must *reframe* our conversation around the church and the "parachurch." In previous chapters, I suggested a definition of the church as well as a new paradigm of "missional extensions" based on what I believe is a biblically rooted functional understanding of the church, instead of the institutional perspective that has dominated our thinking and practice for centuries. Of course, changing a 1,500-year-old paradigm will be difficult and will take time. But we are at another critical moment in church history, and during this reorganizing it is appropriate and necessary to conduct a thorough house-cleaning and to do the necessary rearranging of the assumptions, structures, and practices that are restricting life and growth.

There is a lot of construction going on in my neighborhood these days. The original homes here were built in the 1940s and 1950s as part of the post–World War II housing boom. But those homes can no longer serve the needs of its twenty-first-century residents. In some cases, all that is needed is some updated wiring and plumbing. Perhaps some interior walls need to be moved to restructure the floor plan. In others, owners choose to "pop the top" of small one-story homes, adding another level and extra square footage. For some properties, the only solution is to "scrape" the entire property: to tear down the old house, dig up the old foundation, and start building completely from scratch on an empty lot.

So, too, our reframing of the church will require varying levels of deconstruction, construction, and reconstruction. This is noisy, dusty, dirty, disruptive, time-consuming work, each method costly in its own way. It is also necessary work when old paradigms and frameworks no longer serve current needs.

RESHAPE

Our fourth and final step is to *reshape* our practices. Doing so brings the theoretical and the theological to the ground level of everyday Christian life and ministry. Let me recommend five key actions, with specific questions and suggestions for each, to strengthen and unify the whole church—individual believers, pastors, ministry leaders, and the organizational containers in which we live and labor—for the twenty-first century.

Elevate ecclesiology. No matter where we exist on the missional extension "web," we need to talk more about the nature and purpose of the church. I firmly believe that our lack of attention to ecclesiology has created many of the misunderstandings, false assumptions, and practical problems we are experiencing today.

Pastors and church leaders, when is the last time you taught about the church—not just *your* church, but *the* church, and how your congregation relates to the whole, both locally and globally? Do you make it a priority to regularly cast a kingdom vision for the church among both new and long-time attendees? Does your "functional" theology (your actual ministry practice) match your "espoused" theology (what you say you believe)?

Nonprofit leaders, do you have a clear and coherent ecclesiology? When is the last time *you* taught about the church to your constituents? How do you orient your volunteers and leaders to your ministry's role and relationships with the church?

And lay leaders and everyday Christians, can you articulate a clear understanding of the church and how its various forms should relate to one another? Have you claimed your *identity* as the church, the body of Christ?

Update our vocabulary. Along with our efforts to elevate ecclesiology, it's time to clarify and update our terminology. We've seen that the term *church* has taken on multiple meanings, the majority of them unhelpful or even downright inaccurate, while the term *parachurch* also brings significant confusion and baggage. The missional extensions terminology, on the other hand, clarifies both an overall paradigm and the understanding of each individual's or organization's role within such a functional framework, eliminating the institution-centric perspective that has led to territorialism and competition.

In addition to changing the church-parachurch paradigm and language, we also need to reframe how we talk about the local church. Words matter and shape our understanding. We must therefore sharpen and clarify how we talk about the local church, the gathered *ekklēsia*. For example, what if instead of saying, "I *go to* First Community Church," we said, "I *belong to* First Community Church." Just one word completely changes the meaning of the sentence and the understanding of the nature of the local congregation, and of the individual believer's relationship to it.

As part of changing our language, we should also use accurate terminology to describe nonprofit organizations. There are some nonprofit organizations that are "church-mimicking" to the point where they should be called churches, should identify themselves as churches, and should commit to operating as fully-functioning gatherings of the body—or else determine how they are distinct from a local congregation.

For example, a university campus ministry that gathers weekly for worship, baptizes its "members," holds regular discipleship groups, and equips and sends students on mission trips is probably, by the definition discussed earlier in this book, a church. It doesn't matter that you don't call it a church simply because you don't want to offend local pastors. As Mikey Lynch writes, "Like the distinction between a hobby and a business, there comes a point where a parachurch is distinguishable from a local church in name only."[2]

At the same time, not every organization that claims to be a church is functioning as a church. We need to conduct an honest evaluation of our language and our behaviors, and make sure they reflect reality and consistency. Let's call things what they really are.

Equip and release laity. I have no doubt that most church and nonprofit leaders espouse the values of equipping and releasing laity, but our practices speak otherwise. Churches talk about "every member ministry," but that often means within their organizational boundaries to build or expand their own entity. Similarly, the communication from many nonprofit organizations reflects a belief that *their* need or particular area of ministry is the most important or urgent.

But what if, as ministry leaders, we held our needs and our resources with an open hand and sincerely trusted the Holy Spirit to guide each person? What if we focused on helping believers to differentiate the voice of the Spirit from the many others—ours included—shouting for their time and attention, to identify their own missional calling, and to obey that calling for the good of the kingdom, wherever that may take them?

In my multiple decades of ministry and congregational involvement, I can't recall any situation in which leaders emphasized helping me learn to discern the voice of the Holy Spirit in my own life so that I could discover and follow my unique calling. Instead, they usually told me what was needed, that it was very important, and why and how I should help. Similarly, I don't remember ever receiving a solicitation letter from a nonprofit saying, "We know there are multiple needs around the world, and you have many opportunities to give. We are praying with you and trusting that the Lord will direct you, wherever that may be, as you seek to steward the resources he has given you. Here are some questions to help you discern what that might be."

In addition, how would a "movemental" perspective, instead of a fixed or institutional perspective, affect how we approach lay equipping and leadership development? What if we operated under the assumption that people would be with us for only a few years and no more? What if we decreased or even did away with the strong clergy-laity divide that has developed over centuries of church history? Perhaps that would help us hold less tightly to everything and everyone we currently think of as "ours." The reality is that we are only temporary stewards. Let's increase our release.

Redesign structures. Sam Metcalf and others are right in saying that current local church structures are often not conducive to apostolic activity. But perhaps the real problem is that we have an incorrect imagination and practice of church.

There are a number of believers, communities, and networks around the world that are experimenting with different ways of doing and being church from a missional extension perspective. In addition, at the local gathering level, there is surging interest in what are called "micro-churches," including dinner churches, house churches, table communities, "underground" networks, and many other types of smaller gatherings, the majority of which do not own buildings or require any of the other infrastructure or costs that have become assumed components of an institutional church paradigm.

We also have much to learn from our brothers and sisters around the world who are doing ministry from the margins or under persecution instead of from positions of power, priority, or privilege. I used to think the church in China was disadvantaged because it was not able to exist as an above-ground institution and had to operate as an underground network of house churches, and that churches in poor countries just needed more financial resources. ("Those poor people, if only they could do things like we do." I own it, I confess it—and it was the message I was steeped in for decades.) Today I humbly realize there is so much we need to learn from Christians around the world who are not centered within institutional structures and the trappings of prosperity.

Speaking of which, as a part of this structural redesign, we need to reimagine our financial models and practices. We have looked at the significant needs around the world and the disparity among the haves and the have-nots. Sadly, these disparities are true even in the body of Christ. My brothers and sisters, *this ought not be.* We—*all* of us—must begin taking steps *now* to right our wrongs as it pertains to our views and use of money and material resources. As Ron Sider, John Perkins, Wayne Gordon, and F. Albert Tizon wrote:

> Gripped by the biblical vision of economic and multiethnic *koinonia*, we ultimately cannot condone these divides in our churches. Think about it: The haves flock together in prosperity while the have-nots remain empty-handed in the body of Christ, and black, white, and brown people redeemed in Christ segregate for worship and ministry. We suspect that Moses, the prophets, Jesus, Peter, Paul, and the whole cloud of biblical witnesses would have something to say about this![3]

If Christ called you to account today about how you have stewarded the wealth that has been entrusted to you and to your ministry, would you be able to honestly report that you obeyed God's commands and principles regarding money and caring for the least of these in your organization, your community, and your world?

Commit to collaboration. Under the *missio Dei*, we are all on the same team. We must therefore commit to working together, rejecting territorialism or individualism and instead preaching and practicing unity as members of the same body. Local congregations should prioritize kingdom collaboration over their own ecclesial expansion. Nonprofits should hold pastors and congregations in high esteem, seeking their well-being. Share your own resources generously. Be aware of and celebrate the work of other missional extensions within your community.

It has long been said that "evangelicalism has no pope," meaning there is no central authority to adjudicate or coordinate between expressions of the church. In this absence, collaborative associations, guilds, and meta-networks such as EveryCampus, Lausanne, the Association of Theological Schools, Christian Camping International, the Evangelical Christian Publishers Association, and Exponential—among many others—play a key role, helping to facilitate cooperation and unity and focusing on shared mission rather than doctrinal differences.

Above all, remain connected to one another. In a missional extension framework, we are not just a collection of independent stops or outposts. We are a body, *the* body of Christ. So far as it depends on you, create and foster connection between each member of that body.

SENDING FORTH

My dear brothers and sisters, thank you for joining me through this book. I hope it has been both challenging and encouraging to you, and that you have increased in your understanding of and love for the church.

My classroom epiphany many years ago, when I first asked, "What is the church?" has changed the course of my professional life and my everyday practice as both a ministry leader and a follower of Jesus Christ. The Lord has nurtured in me a deep, abiding love and hope in his body, the church. I have a new appreciation for *all* expressions of the body of Christ, and I love hearing how God is at work around the world through all types of ministry structures. And I am passionate about instilling that love and appreciation in the ministry leaders I am blessed to work with.

My deeper, broader understanding of the church has caused me (along with my husband) to rethink our giving, our volunteering, even our vocations. For our charitable giving, we have become more intentional as to how much we give and where. Instead of responding to every request for donations, we have developed a list of our values, and organizations that share those values. In addition to giving to our local church and to emerging leaders as they get started in vocational ministry, we realized we wanted to do more to help meet needs in our local community. A search of area organizations and their work led us to donate regularly to our neighborhood elementary school, which serves a wide cross-section of families in the community through a food bank housed in its basement. We remain open to giving to other outlets as the Lord leads. We have also started to ask more pointed questions about how our money is being used by an organization, and whether it is effectively being channeled to missional needs and purposes.

We also realized the need to determine priorities for where we give our time; we simply couldn't accept every invitation or meet every need, although we've had to work through the guilt we have sometimes felt in disappointing others when we say no to a request.

My husband has clearly been called to serve the *ekklēsia*, the local congregation, through pastoral and preaching ministry, and now also by teaching those things to the next generation of ministry leaders. Meanwhile, I am called to serve the church more broadly by developing and encouraging leaders who serve in a variety of ministry contexts. My role as a teacher, writer, and shepherd to these leaders is to ask questions, to challenge what might be flawed assumptions and understandings, and to propose new ways of thinking about the church and doing ministry.

I pray that the conversation in this book has spurred greater love and deeper thought in you as well. As members of Christ's body, let each of us commit today to working together toward a renewed, unified, apostolic church. And let us join together in praying this collect for the mission of the church:

> O God of all the nations of the earth: Remember the multitudes who have been created in your image but have not known the redeeming work of our Savior Jesus Christ; and grant that, by the prayers and labors of your holy Church, they may be brought to know and worship you as you have been revealed in your Son; who lives and reigns with you and the Holy Spirit, one God, for ever and ever. Amen.[4]

ACKNOWLEDGMENTS

This book is the product of years of reflection, conversation, and personal and team effort. I'd like to thank as many contributors to that process as I can, and as I can remember.

In the fall of 2019 I taught a new Doctor of Ministry course I designed for Denver Seminary titled "Reclaiming Ecclesiology: Faithful Foundations for Effective Ministry." The thirteen students who served as my guinea pigs in this new course helped immeasurably to refine my thinking about the things written in this book. Thank you to Brandon, Luke B., Liz, Clayton, Rick, Trudy, Jodi, Jason J., Jacob, Jeron, Rodney, Sue, and Paul for our fantastic class and our continuing conversations over the years.

A special thanks goes to Dr. Clayton Dye, one of the aforementioned students who took my course and this topic and ran with it for his doctoral thesis and far beyond and is leading the way in the ecclesiological conversation as it applies to missionaries on college campuses. Clayton, I have learned so much from our discussions and from your research, much of which is reflected (and appropriately cited!) in this book. It is a great honor to claim you as one of my students and now as a friend and ministry colleague.

What became a lifelong interest in the church and parachurch was first animated when I was a master's student at Denver Seminary many years ago. Thanks to Dr. Bruce Shelley for his original "Church and Parachurch" course that served as the inspiration for my DMin course, and to his protégés, Dr. Scott Wenig and Dr. Marshall Shelley, who passed along Bruce's passion to countless numbers of students over multiple decades. Scott, thank you for the stimulating conversations and teaching that helped shape my thinking when I was your student, then friend, then also colleague. Marshall, thank you for giving me the chance to teach a DMin course in your father's footsteps and for your constant encouragement and empowerment of my writing and teaching.

To Denver Seminary and Dr. Don Payne, thank you for the opportunity to serve as director of the Doctor of Ministry program, which affords me the privilege of working on a daily basis with some of the most amazingly bright, talented, and gracious colleagues, and serving and learning from the most incredible ministry practitioners serving in all types of contexts around the world. Denver Seminary is a special place, and I'm grateful to be able to give back in small measure to the alma mater from which I have so greatly received.

Thanks to Jerry White for taking the time and risk to write *The Church and the Parachurch* back in 1983 and for continuing to champion the importance of church-parachurch conversation and partnership. Jerry, it is an immense honor and privilege to carry forward the work you started. Thank you for your blessing and encouragement.

The inaugural Church-Parachurch Leaders' Summit that I mention in this book has now been followed by several more gatherings around the country. To Scott Harris, thank you for your vision and unbelievable energy around this topic and for your gifts of gathering and connecting like-minded leaders. Thanks also to those who have attended and who continue to further the dialogue on this issue.

Thank you also to everyone who has enthusiastically engaged in personal conversations with me, challenging and shaping my ideas about the church and parachurch. This includes but is certainly not limited to Eugene Kim, Rowland Smith, Sam Metcalf, Bob Blincoe, Tim and Sarah Koller, David Buschart, James Rider, Ryan Tafilowski, Jayne Wilcox, Eric and Jodi Nevins, Lewis Crouse, Barb Russo, John Moreland, Chuck and Katie Fowler, Taylor Ward, Jim and Lori Gustafson, Jamison Ward, Mikey Lynch, John Pellowe, Craig and Fran Blomberg, Rick Dunn, Harv Powers, Shawn Allen, J. D. Kim, and countless others. I apologize for any omissions due to my middle-aged recall, or the lack thereof. And special thanks to the many wonderful folks at Forge America and Missio Alliance who have helped me realize I'm not crazy in my questions and thinking—or that at least I'm not crazy all by myself.

To Harv Powers and Rick Dunn, I am continually grateful for our Nile Mastermind and the ways you both have challenged and strengthened me to be a more courageous leader and truth-teller.

I have now taught Reclaiming Ecclesiology several times, and each group of students has helped me sharpen my thinking, as I hope I have done for them. Thank you to those students for taking my class and for engaging so wholeheartedly with the coursework, with your classmates, and with me. It's an honor to learn with you. Thanks also to the broader Denver Seminary DMin community and to my students at previous institutions including those at Lancaster Bible College and Capital Seminary & Graduate School.

Al Hsu of InterVarsity Press immediately caught and championed the vision for this book. Al, thank you for bringing me into the IVP family and for bringing your churchman's heart and expert editorial eye to this book. The IVP team has been a joy to work with from start to finish; thanks to Lori Neff not only for your unique skills but also for reflecting a Christlike spirit and sharing constant encouragement all along the way.

As always, thank you to Keely Boeving and the other great folks at WordServe Literary for your fantastic representation and ongoing support.

I reserve my deepest love and gratitude for Dave, my First Person, my life partner, my constant strength and support, and my greatest champion and encourager. A few words in this space could never fully express my joy and thankfulness for nearly thirty years of marriage and ministry together, which has included countless conversations about the church, leadership, and ministry since we were seminary students. It's amazing and beautiful that we have come full circle together, back to Denver where it all started. God is good and I love how we are married.

And last but not least, I must give thanks and a few extra treats to Brewster, my sweet beagle, who has now faithfully served as canine companion and chief cuddler, whether at my feet, by my side, or in my lap, for six books and hopefully counting.

NOTES

I. WHY THIS BOOK?

[1]Darrell L. Guder, ed., *Missional Church: A Vision for the Sending of the Church in North America* (Grand Rapids, MI: Eerdmans, 1998), 3.

[2]In 2023 Australian research and ministry leader Mikey Lynch restarted the conversation with his fine book *The Vine Movement: Supporting Gospel Growth Beyond Your Church* (Youngstown, OH: Matthias Media, 2022).

2. WHERE ARE WE?

[1]Phyllis Tickle, *The Great Emergence: How Christianity Is Changing and Why* (Grand Rapids, MI: Baker Books, 2012), 10.

[2]Tickle, *The Great Emergence,* 10.

[3]Jeffrey M. Jones, "U.S. Church Membership Falls Below Majority for First Time," *Gallup,* March 29, 2021, https://news.gallup.com/poll/341963/church -membership-falls-below-majority-first-time.aspx.

[4]David Roach, "Southern Baptists Lost Nearly Half a Million Members Last Year," *Christianity Today,* May 12, 2023, www.christianitytoday.com/news/2023 /may/southern-baptist-membership-drop-baptism-rebound-sbc.html.

[5]Bob Smietana, *Reorganized Religion: The Reshaping of the American Church and Why It Matters* (New York: Worthy, 2023), 106.

[6]Scott Neuman, "The Faithful See Both Crisis and Opportunity as Churches Close Across the Country," *NPR,* May 17, 2023, www.npr.org/2023/05/17 /1175452002/church-closings-religious-affiliation.

[7]Gregory A. Smith et al., "Religious 'Nones' in America: Who They Are and What They Believe," Pew Research Center, January 24, 2024, www.pewresearch .org/religion/2024/01/24/religious-nones-in-america-who-they-are-and -what-they-believe/.

[8]Kate Shellnutt, "Above Reproach? Fewer Americans See Pastors as Ethical," *Christianity Today,* January 25, 2024, www.christianitytoday.com/news

/2024/january/pastor-trust-credibility-reputation-gallup-poll-clergy-ethi
.html.

9 Jim David and Michael Graham, *The Great Dechurching* (Grand Rapids, MI: Zondervan, 2023), 3.

10 Christopher P. Scheitle, *Beyond the Congregation: The World of Christian Nonprofits* (Oxford: Oxford University Press, 2010).

11 Smietana, *Reorganizing Religion,* 18.

12 Justin Brierley, "A Christian Revival Is Under Way in Britain," *The Spectator,* March 30, 2024, www.spectator.co.uk/article/a-christian-revival-is-under-way-in-britain/.

13 "The State of Church Membership: Trends and Statistics [2024]," *Churchtrac,* accessed October 14, 2024, www.churchtrac.com/articles/the-state-of-church-membership.

14 Scheitle, *Beyond the Congregation,* 182.

15 Staff Reporter, "A Quarter of UK Charities are 'Faith-based,'" *Church Times,* April 29, 2016, www.churchtimes.co.uk/articles/2016/29-april/news/uk/a-quarter-of-uk-charities-are-faith-based.

16 Wesley K. Willmer, J. David Schmidt, and Martyn Smith, *The Prospering Parachurch: Enlarging the Boundaries of God's Kingdom* (San Francisco: Jossey-Bass, 1998), 201-14.

17 Scheitle, *Beyond the Congregation,* 174.

18 Peter Greer and Chris Horst, *Rooting for Rivals: How Collaboration and Generosity Increase the Impact of Leaders, Charities, and Churches* (Bloomington, MN: Bethany House, 2018), 52-53.

19 Philanthropy Roundtable, "Who Gives Most to Charity?," accessed February 24, 2024, www.philanthropyroundtable.org/almanac/who-gives-most-to-charity.

20 Sam Rainer, "Churches Are Receiving Less of Total Charitable Giving," *Outreach Magazine,* March 6, 2023, https://outreachmagazine.com/features/74316-churches-are-receiving-less-of-total-charitable-giving.html.

21 Rainer, "Churches Are Receiving Less of Total Charitable Giving."

22 Daniel X. Matz, "Generational Change in Giving and Philanthropy," *Candid,* November 8, 2023, https://blog.candid.org/post/next-generation-donors-future-philanthropy/.

23 UNHCR, "Refugee Data Finder," United Nations, October 24, 2023, www.unhcr.org/refugee-statistics/.

24 Andrea Peer, "Global Poverty: Facts, FAQs, and How to Help," *World Vision,* April 4, 2023, www.worldvision.org/sponsorship-news-stories/global-poverty-facts.

25 The Traveling Team, "Missions Stats: The Current State of the World," accessed October 14, 2024, www.thetravelingteam.org/stats.

[26] David J. Bosch, *Transforming Mission: Paradigm Shifts in Theology of Mission*, American Society of Missiology Series Book 16 (Maryknoll, NY: Orbis Books, 2011), 375.

[27] Bosch, *Transforming Mission*, 375.

[28] Tickle, *The Great Emergence*, 11.

3. HOW DID THIS ALL START?

[1] Frederick J. Cwiekowski, *The Beginnings of the Church* (Mahwah, NJ: Paulist Press, 1988), 77.

[2] Cwiekowski, *The Beginnings of the Church*, 150.

[3] John Foxe, *Foxe's Book of Martyrs* (Public domain, first printed 1563), 3-4.

[4] Andrew B. McGowan, *Ancient Christian Worship: Early Church Practices in Social, Historical, and Theological Perspective* (Grand Rapids, MI: Baker Academic, 2014), 5-6.

[5] Bruce Shelley with Marshall Shelley, *Church History in Plain Language*, 5th ed. (Grand Rapids, MI: Zondervan Academic, 2021), 82.

[6] Cwiekowski, *The Beginnings of the Church*, 183.

[7] Robert Blincoe, "Separate Administrative Structures for Church and Mission: Paul and Barnabas Led 'Field Governed' Missionary Bands," *Lighthouse and Flint* (blog), September 13, 2022, https://robertblincoe.blog/separate-administrative-structures-for-church-and-mission-4th-of-7-paul-and-barnabas-led-a-field-governed-missionary-band/.

[8] David Bosch, *Transforming Mission: Paradigm Shifts in Theology of Mission*, American Society of Missiology Series Book 16 (Maryknoll, NY: Orbis Books, 2011), 206.

[9] Cwiekowski, *The Beginnings of the Church*, 190-91.

[10] Cwiekowski, *The Beginnings of the Church*, 191.

[11] Shelley, *Church History in Plain Language*, 152.

[12] Benedict of Nursia, *The Rule of St. Benedict*, trans. Rev. Boniface Verheyen, OSB (Atchison, KS: PlanetMonk Books, 2011–2018), 84.

[13] Robert Louis Wilken, *The First Thousand Years: A Global History of Christianity* (New Haven, CT: Yale University Press, 2012), 107.

[14] Shelley, *Church History in Plain Language*, 157.

[15] Shelley, *Church History in Plain Language*, 238.

[16] C. H. Lawrence, *Medieval Monasticism: Forms of Religious Life in Western Europe in the Middle Ages*, 3rd ed. (Essex, UK: Pearson Education Ltd., 2001), 123.

[17] Robert Tombs, *The English and Their History* (New York: Vintage Books, 2014), 98.

[18] Timothy S. Miller, "Basil's House of Healing," *Christian History*, no. 101, 14.

[19] Lawrence, *Medieval Monasticism*, 14.

[20]Tombs, *The English and Their History*, 171.

[21]Wilken, *The First Thousand Years*, 261.

[22]Norman Tanner, *A New Short History of the Catholic Church* (New York: Bloomsbury Continuum, 2011), 124.

[23]Wilken, *The First Thousand Years*, 105.

[24]Patricia Wittberg, *The Rise and Decline of Catholic Religious Orders: A Social Movement Perspective* (Albany, NY: State University of New York Press, 1994), 75.

[25]Tanner, *A New Short History of the Catholic Church*, 72.

[26]Shelley, *Church History in Plain Language*, 251.

[27]Tanner, *A New Short History of the Catholic Church*, 124.

[28]Bosch, *Transforming Mission*, 235.

[29]Shelley, *Church History in Plain Language*, 241.

[30]Tanner, *A New Short History of the Catholic Church*, 187.

[31]Tanner, *A New Short History of the Catholic Church*, 180.

4. HOW DID WE GET HERE?

[1]David J. Bosch, *Transforming Mission: Paradigm Shifts in Theology of Mission*, American Society of Missiology Series Book 16 (Maryknoll, NY: Orbis Books, 2011), 250.

[2]Bosch, *Transforming Mission*, 335.

[3]Andrew Pettegree, *Brand Luther: How an Unheralded Monk Turned His Small Town Into a Center of Publishing, Made Himself the Most Famous Man in Europe—and Started the Protestant Reformation* (New York: Penguin Books, 2015), 23.

[4]Bruce Shelley with Marshall Shelley, *Church History in Plain Language*, 5th ed. (Grand Rapids, MI: Zondervan Academic, 2021), 360.

[5]Bosch, *Transforming Mission*, 336.

[6]Christopher P. Scheitle, *Beyond the Congregation: The World of Christian Non-profits* (Oxford: Oxford University Press, 2010), 21.

[7]Scheitle, *Beyond the Congregation*, 21.

[8]Randall Balmer, *Evangelicalism in America* (Waco, TX: Baylor University Press, 2016), 25.

[9]Shelley, *Church History in Plain Language*, 429.

[10]Shelley, *Church History in Plain Language*, 436.

[11]Shirley Rollinson, "A Brief History of Denominations," April 23, 2019, www.drshirley.org/hist/hist21-denominations.html.

[12]Paul Arnsberger et al., "A History of the Tax-Exempt Sector: An SOI Perspective," *Statistics of Income Bulletin* (Winter 2008), www.irs.gov/pub/irs-soi/tehistory.pdf.

[13] Balmer, *Evangelicalism in America,* 36.

[14] Balmer, *Evangelicalism in America,* x.

[15] Robert Wuthnow, *The Restructuring of American Religion: Society and Faith Since World War II* (Princeton, NJ: Princeton University Press, 1988), 113, 101.

[16] Hartford Institute, "Megachurch Definition," Hartford Institute for Religion Research, http://hirr.hartsem.edu/megachurch/definition.html.

[17] Mike Cosper, "Boomers, the Big Sort, and Really, Really Big Churches," prod. Mike Cosper, *The Rise and Fall of Mars Hill,* podcast, 58:11, June 28, 2021, www.christianitytoday.com/ct/podcasts/rise-and-fall-of-mars-hill /mars-hill-podcast-boomers-big-sort-hybels-warren-driscoll.html.

[18] Scott Thumma, "What Makes God Free Is Free Indeed: Nondenominational Identity and Its Networks of Support," Hartford Institute for Religion Research, 1999, www.hartfordinstitute.org/bookshelf/thumma_article5.html.

[19] Jerry White, "Current Realities," talk presented at Church-Parachurch Summit, Denver, CO, October 31, 2022.

[20] Scheitle, *Beyond the Congregation,* 28.

[21] Dean R. Hoge, Benton Johnson, and Donald A. Luidens, "Types of Denominational Switching Among Protestant Young Adults," *Journal for the Scientific Study of Religion* 34, no. 2 (June 1995): 253.

[22] Scheitle, *Beyond the Congregation,* 30.

[23] Norman Tanner, *A New Short History of the Catholic Church* (New York: Bloomsbury Continuum, 2011), 224.

[24] Pope Paul VI, *Apostolicam Actuositatem,* November 18, 1965, Vatican City.

[25] I am riffing off of missiologist David Bosch's statement that "the gospel always comes to people in cultural robes." Bosch, *Transforming Mission,* 304.

[26] Bosch, *Transforming Mission,* 187.

[27] Scheitle, *Beyond the Congregation,* 35.

5. WHAT IS THE CHURCH?

[1] Yes, we're still going to get to whether this is even the right word, and whether church and parachurch are separate things. Stick with me.

[2] I wish I could say "lectern" or "podium" as that would sound way more distinguished, but we know how these gatherings really work.

[3] Terry Ishee and Angie Ward, "Loaded Terms," *The Big C Church Podcast,* August 22, 2023, https://angiewardphd.com/loaded-terms-with-terry -ishee-the-big-c-church-podcast-ep-1/.

[4] Johannes P. Louw and Eugene A. Nida, eds., *Greek-English Lexicon of the New Testament Based on Semantic Domains,* vol. 1, 2nd ed. (New York: United Bible Societies, 1989), 126.

⁵Colin Brown, ed., "Church, Synagogue," *The New International Dictionary of New Testament Theology,* vol. 1 (Grand Rapids, MI: Zondervan, 1986), 297-98.

⁶Mark Dever, *The Church: The Gospel Made Visible* (Nashville, TN: B&H Academic, 2012), 8.

⁷I'm guilty myself, as I host a podcast called "The Big C Church."

⁸John Alesandro, "The Origins of the Phrase 'Universal Church,'" March 17, 2016, www.ulc.org/universal-church-origins.

⁹Brown, "Church, Synagogue," 299.

¹⁰Earl D. Radmacher, *The Nature of the Church* (Nicholasville, KY: Schmul Publishing Co., 1996).

¹¹Louw and Nida, *Greek-English Lexicon,* 126.

¹²Brown, "Church, Synagogue," 299.

¹³D. W. B. Robinson, "Church," in *New Bible Dictionary,* 3rd ed., ed. I. Howard Marshall (Downers Grove, IL: InterVarsity Press, 1996), 200.

¹⁴Louw and Nida, *Greek-English Lexicon,* 126.

¹⁵Howard A. Snyder, *The Community of the King* (Downers Grove, IL: InterVarsity Press, 1977), 59.

¹⁶Dever, *The Church,* 12.

¹⁷Millard J. Erickson, *Christian Theology,* 3rd ed. (Grand Rapids, MI: Baker Academic, 2013), 1127.

¹⁸Eugene Kim and Angie Ward, "What is the Church? Part 5," *The Big C Church Podcast,* November 20, 2023, https://angiewardphd.com/what-is-the-church-part-5-with-eugene-kim-the-big-c-church-podcast-ep-14/.

6. WHAT DOES THE CHURCH DO?

¹David J. Bosch, *Transforming Mission: Paradigm Shifts in Theology of Mission,* American Society of Missiology Series Book 16 (Maryknoll, NY: Orbis Books, 2011), 505.

²Bosch, *Transforming Mission,* 402.

³Leo Rowland Smith, *Missional Emergence: How* Missio Dei *and Its Intersection with Transformative Learning Theory Can Move Christ-Followers Toward a Missional Lifestyle.* (Ph.D. diss., Fuller Theological Seminary, 2023), 28.

⁴Bosch, *Transforming Mission,* 401.

⁵Bosch, *Transforming Mission,* 403.

⁶Bosch, *Transforming Mission,* 504.

⁷Bosch, *Transforming Mission,* 505.

⁸Frances Fulling Blomberg, *Forming and Sustaining Christian Community in a Consumer Culture: An Analysis of and Search for Appropriate Models* (Ph.D. diss., University of Wales/International Baptist Theological Seminary, 2014), 184-85.

[9] Mark Dever, *The Church: The Gospel Made Visible* (Nashville, TN: B&H Academic, 2012), 13.

[10] As David Bosch wrote, "There can be no doubt that social justice was at the very heart of the prophetic tradition of the Old Testament" (Bosch, *Transforming Mission*, 410).

[11] Jürgen Moltmann, *The Church in the Power of the Spirit* (New York: Harper and Row, 1977), 64.

[12] Thomas H. Eriksen, *What Is Anthropology?*, eds. Thomas H. Eriksen and Jon P. Mitchell (London: Pluto Press, 2004), 101.

[13] Joann Keyton, *Communication and Organizational Culture: A Key to Understanding Work Experiences* (Thousand Oaks, CA: Sage Publications, 2005), 6.

[14] Stephen P. Robbins, *Organization Theory: The Structure and Design of Organizations* (Englewood Cliffs, NJ: Prentice-Hall, 1983), 6.

[15] Edward W. Klink, III, *The Local Church: What It Is and Why It Matters for Every Christian* (Wheaton, IL: Crossway, 2021), 22, 25.

[16] Klink, *The Local Church,* 23.

[17] Ryan Tafilowski and Angie Ward, "What is the Church? Part 1," *The Big C Church Podcast,* October 24, 2023, https://angiewardphd.com/what-is-the-church-part-1-with-ryan-tafilowski-the-big-c-church-podcast-ep-10/.

[18] Dulles uses a capital "C" when referring to the church, speaking of the collective body of Christ around the world.

[19] Avery Dulles, *Models of the Church* (New York: Image Books, 2002), 45-46.

[20] Dulles, *Models of the Church,* 71.

[21] John Calvin, *The Institutes of the Christian Religion,* book 4, chapter 1 (Grand Rapids, MI: Eerdmans Printing Company, Reprinted November 1983), 289.

[22] Underground Network, "How It Works," accessed December 27, 2023, www.undergroundnetwork.org/how-it-works-index.

[23] Michael Beck, "The Blended Ecology," Missio Alliance Awakenings, 2019, https://s3.amazonaws.com/awakenings2019/Audio/Workshops/10_BlendedEcology_Beck.mp3.

[24] Personal files of author.

[25] Mikey Lynch, *The Vine Movement: Supporting Gospel Growth Beyond Your Church* (Sydney, Australia: Matthias Media, 2023), 63.

[26] Personal conversation with author.

[27] Jerry White, *The Church & The Parachurch: An Uneasy Marriage* (Portland, OR: Multnomah, 1983), 73.

[28] Gregg R. Allison, *Sojourners and Strangers: The Doctrine of the Church* (Wheaton, IL: Crossway, 2012), 28.

[29] Glenn Collins, "What Does APEST Look Like in Community?" (Does the Church Have a Future and a Hope?, part 4), FŌS Church, June 13,

2022, https://fos.church/conversation-notes/ydkmn-sexmc-4cz2h-gc2tp
-e9cmz-f7s2k-m85s7-wdk4s.

7. WHERE DO WE STAND WITH ONE ANOTHER?

[1]Stephen Board, "The Great Evangelical Power Shift," *Eternity*, June 1979, 17.

[2]Board, "The Great Evangelical Power Shift," 17.

[3]"What Is a Nonprofit?" National Council of Nonprofits, accessed January 29, 2024, www.councilofnonprofits.org/what-nonprofit.

[4]Joann Keyton, *Communication and Organizational Culture: A Key to Understanding Work Experiences* (Thousand Oaks, CA: Sage Publications, 2005), 7.

[5]J. Alan Youngren, "Parachurch Proliferation: The Frontier Spirit Caught in Traffic," *Christianity Today*, November 6, 1981, www.christianitytoday.com /ct/1981/november-6/parachurch-proliferation-frontier-spirit-caught-in -traffic.html.

[6]B. L. Shelley, "Parachurch Groups (Voluntary Societies)," in *Dictionary of Christianity in America,* ed. Daniel G. Reid (Downers Grove, IL: InterVarsity Press, 1990), 863.

[7]Mikey Lynch, *The Vine Movement: Supporting Gospel Growth Beyond Your Church* (Sydney, Australia: Matthias Media, 2023), 54.

[8]Wesley K. Willmer, J. David Schmidt, and Martyn Smith, *The Prospering Parachurch: Enlarging the Boundaries of God's Kingdom* (San Francisco: Jossey-Bass, 1998), 14.

[9]Christopher P. Scheitle, *Beyond the Congregation: The World of Christian Nonprofits* (Oxford, UK: Oxford University Press, 2010), 71.

[10]Scheitle, *Beyond the Congregation,* 33.

[11]Jerry White, *The Church & the Parachurch: An Uneasy Marriage* (Portland, OR: Multnomah, 1983), 19.

[12]The six theological perspectives are drawn from White, *The Church & the Parachurch*, 65-66, and used with express permission from Jerry White.

[13]A notable exception is those affiliated with the 9Marks organization founded by Reformed theologian and pastor Mark Dever. For 9Marks, the role of the parachurch is "to protect the church." See J. Mack Stiles, "Nine Marks of a Healthy Parachurch Ministry," 9Marks, March 1, 2011, www.9marks.org /article/journalnine-marks-healthy-parachurch-ministry/.

[14]Ralph Winter, "The Two Structures of God's Redemptive Mission," *Missiology: An International Review* 2, no. 1 (January 1974): 127.

[15]Sam Metcalf, *Beyond the Local Church: How Apostolic Movements Can Change the World* (Downers Grove, IL: InterVarsity Press, 2016), 29-30.

[16]Winter, "The Two Structures of God's Redemptive Mission," 131.

[17]Winter, "The Two Structures of God's Redemptive Mission," 224. From a later version of the article: www.undertheiceberg.com/wp-content/uploads /2006/04/Sodality-Winter%20on%20Two%20Structures1.pdf.

[18]Metcalf, *Beyond the Local Church,* 21.

[19]Metcalf, *Beyond the Local Church,* 54.

[20]Metcalf, *Beyond the Local Church,* 43.

[21]Robert Blincoe, "Galatians 2:7-10 Paul and Peter Shake Hands, Recognizing Two Administrations of the Gospel," *Lighthouse and Flint* (blog), July 26, 2022, https://robertblincoe.blog/paul-and-peter-resolve-a-problem-their -differences-with-a-handshake/.

[22]Mikey Lynch, *The Vine Movement: Supporting Gospel Growth Beyond Your Church* (Sydney, Australia: Matthias Media, 2023), 67.

[23]A. F. Walls, "Apostle," in *New Bible Dictionary*, 3rd ed., I. Howard Marshall, ed., (Downers Grove, IL: InterVarsity Press, 1996), 59.

[24]Alan Hirsch and Tim Catchim, *The Permanent Revolution: Apostolic Imagination and Practice for the 21st Century* (San Francisco: Jossey-Bass, 2012), xvi.

[25]Roland Allen, *The Spontaneous Expansion of the Church: And the Causes Which Hinder It* (Cambridge, UK: Lutterworth Press, 2006), 96.

[26]Edmund P. Clowney, *The Church: Contours of Christian Theology* (Downers Grove, IL: InterVarsity Press, 1995), 207.

[27]Clayton Dye, "The College Missionary's Place in a Formal Ecclesiology" (D.Min. thesis, Denver Seminary, 2023), 20-21, 108.

[28]Scheitle, *Beyond the Congregation,* 4.

[29]Scheitle, *Beyond the Congregation,* 42.

[30]Lesslie Newbigin, *Sign of the Kingdom* (Grand Rapids, MI: Wm. B. Eerdmans, 1981), 41.

[31]Lynch, *The Vine Movement,* 76.

[32]Lynch, *The Vine Movement,* 81, 78.

[33]Lynch, *The Vine Movement,* 166.

[34]First Corinthians 12, paraphrased by Al Hsu. Email correspondence, June 6, 2024.

8. WHY DON'T WE ALWAYS GET ALONG?

[1]I'm going to keep using this language in the hopes that it catches on.

[2]The University of North Carolina at Greensboro, I'm looking at you.

[3]Alan Hirsch and Tim Catchim, *The Permanent Revolution: Apostolic Imagination and Practice for the 21st Century* (San Francisco: Jossey-Bass, 2012), 227.

[4]Peter Greer and Chris Horst, *Rooting for Rivals: How Collaboration and Generosity Increase the Impact of Leaders, Charities, and Churches* (Bloomington, MN: Bethany House, 2018), 60.

[5]Greer and Horst, *Rooting for Rivals,* 61.

[6]Ryan Burge and Walter Kim, "The Rise and Fall of Institutions," *The NAE Podcast,* October 15, 2023, www.nae.org/burgepodcast/.

[7]Tim Koller and Angie Ward, "A Failure of Leadership," *The Big C Church Podcast,* August 29, 2023, https://angiewardphd.com/a-failure-of-leadership -with-tim-koller-the-big-c-church-podcast-ep-2/.

[8]Greer and Horst, *Rooting for Rivals,* 73, 92.

[9]Christopher P. Scheitle, *Beyond the Congregation: The World of Christian Non- profits* (Oxford, UK: Oxford University Press, 2010), 47-48.

[10]Adapted from Scheitle, *Beyond the Congregation,* 49.

[11]Scheitle, *Beyond the Congregation,* 55.

[12]Scheitle, *Beyond the Congregation,* 37.

[13]Interview with Rowland Smith, December 20, 2023.

[14]Daniel Silliman, "For Sale: Christian Ministry Headquarters," *Christianity Today,* June 2, 2024, www.christianitytoday.com/news/2024/june/remote -work-evangelical-office-headquarters-for-sale.html.

[15]Greer and Horst, *Rooting for Rivals,* 12.

[16]Greer and Horst, *Rooting for Rivals,* 73.

[17]Greer and Horst, *Rooting for Rivals,* 116.

[18]Greer and Horst, *Rooting for Rivals,* 159.

[19]Scheitle, *Beyond the Congregation,* 35.

[20]Zoom conversation with Mikey Lynch, December 21, 2023, and correspon- dence July 31, 2024.

9. HOW CAN WE WORK TOGETHER?

[1]Eugene Kim, Guest Lecture in Reclaiming Ecclesiology, Denver Seminary, January 10, 2024. See also www.newwinecollective.org.

[2]Interview with Rowland Smith, December 20, 2023.

[3]"'Every Campus' Movement Aims to Reach Hundreds of Unreached Colleges for Jesus," CBN News, July 28, 2023, www.youtube.com/watch?v=lV54js -Ykf4.

[4]Lausanne Movement, "The Lausanne Covenant," accessed October 14, 2024, https://lausanne.org/statement/lausanne-covenant.

[5]Mark DeYmaz with Harry Li, *The Coming Revolution in Church Economics: Why Tithes and Offerings Are No Longer Enough, and What You Can Do About It* (Grand Rapids, MI: Baker Books, 2019), 90.

[6]Zoom interview with Mark DeYmaz, December 19, 2023, and Mark DeYmaz with Harry Li, *The Coming Revolution in Church Economics: Why Tithes and Of- ferings Are No Longer Enough, and What You Can Do About It* (Grand Rapids, MI: Baker Books, 2019).

[7]Sue Phillips, "The Spiritual Infrastructure of the Future," *Glean Network*, June 26, 2024, www.gleannetwork.org/post/the-spiritual-infrastructure-of -the-future.

10. WHERE DO WE GO FROM HERE?

[1]Edward W. Klink, III, *The Local Church: What It Is and Why It Matters for Every Christian* (Wheaton, IL: Crossway, 2021), 25.

[2]Mikey Lynch, *The Vine Movement: Supporting Gospel Growth Beyond Your Church* (Sydney, Australia: Matthias Media, 2023), 69.

[3]Ronald J. Sider et al., *Linking Arms, Linking Lives: How Urban-Suburban Partnerships Can Transform Communities* (Grand Rapids, MI: Baker Books, 2008), 64.

[4]"Collect for the Mission of the Church," Book of Common Prayer Online, www .bcponline.org/Collects/variousc.html.

BIBLIOGRAPHY

Alesandro, John. "The Origins of the Phrase 'Universal Church.'" www.ulc.org /universal-church-origins.

Allen, Roland. *The Spontaneous Expansion of the Church: And the Causes Which Hinder It.* Cambridge, UK: Lutterworth Press, 2006.

Allison, Gregg R. *Sojourners and Strangers: The Doctrine of the Church.* Wheaton, IL: Crossway, 2012.

Arakaki, Robert. "Calvin and the 'Fall of the Church.'" Orthodox-Reformed Bridge. January 29, 2014. https://orthodoxbridge.com/2014/01/29/calvin -and-the-fall-of-the-church/.

Arnsberger, Paul, Melissa Ludlum, Margaret Riley, and Mark Stanton. "A History of the Tax-Exempt Sector: An SOI Perspective." *Statistics of Income Bulletin* (Winter 2008). www.irs.gov/pub/irs-soi/tehistory.pdf.

Athenagoras. *A Plea for the Christians.* AD 177. www.newadvent.org/fathers /0205.htm.

Balmer, Randall. *Evangelicalism in America.* Waco, TX: Baylor University Press, 2016.

Barna, George. *Revolution.* Wheaton, IL: Tyndale House Publishers, 2005.

Baylis, Robert H. *A Guide to the Christian Heritage of London.* London: Christian Heritage London, 2021.

Beck, Michael. "The Blended Ecology." Missio Alliance Awakenings 2019. https://s3.amazonaws.com/awakenings2019/Audio/Workshops/10 _BlendedEcology_Beck.mp3.

Benedict of Nursia. *The Rule of St. Benedict,* translated by Rev. Boniface Verheyen, OSB. Atchison, KS: PlanetMonk Books, 2011–2018.

"BGEA History." https://billygraham.org/news/media-resources/electronic -press-kit/bgea-history/.

Bird, Michael. *Evangelical Theology: A Biblical and Systematic Introduction.* 2nd ed. Grand Rapids, MI: Zondervan Academic, 2020.

Blincoe, Robert. "Galatians 2:7-10 Paul and Peter Shake Hands, Recognizing Two Administrations of the Gospel." *Lighthouse and Flint* (blog). July 26,

2022. https://robertblincoe.blog/paul-and-peter-resolve-a-problem-their-differences-with-a-handshake/.

Blincoe, Robert. "Separate Administrative Structures for Church and Mission: Paul and Barnabas Led 'Field Governed' Missionary Bands." *Lighthouse and Flint* (blog). September 13, 2022. https://robertblincoe.blog/separate-administrative-structures-for-church-and-mission-4th-of-7-paul-and-barnabas-led-a-field-governed-missionary-band/.

Blincoe, Robert Alan. "A New Social Contract Relating Missions Societies to Ecclesiastical Structures." Ph.D. diss., William Carey International University, 2012.

Blincoe, Robert A. "Relating Church Hierarchies to Mission Agencies: Healing a Breach in the Protestant Church." *Evangelical and Frontier Mission: Perspectives on the Global Progress of the Gospel* 9 (2011): 163–80.

Blincoe, Robert A. "The Strange Structure of Mission Agencies, Part I: Still Two Structures After All These Years?" *International Journal of Frontier Missions* 19, no. 1 (Spring 2002): 5–8.

Blomberg, Craig L. *Matthew*. The New American Commentary, vol. 22. Nashville, TN: Broadman Press, 1992.

Blomberg, Frances Fulling. *Forming and Sustaining Christian Community in a Consumer Culture: An Analysis of and Search for Appropriate Models*. Ph.D. diss., University of Wales/International Baptist Theological Seminary, 2014.

Board, Stephen. "The Great Evangelical Power Shift." *Eternity* (June 1979), 16–21.

Boice, James Montgomery. *Foundations of the Christian Faith: A Comprehensive and Readable Theology*. Downers Grove, IL: IVP Academic, 2019.

Bosch, David J. *Transforming Mission: Paradigm Shifts in Theology of Mission.* 20th Anniversary Ed. American Society of Missiology Series Book 16. Maryknoll, NY: Orbis Books, 2011.

Brierley, Justin. "A Christian Revival Is Under Way in Britain." *The Spectator.* March 30, 2024. www.spectator.co.uk/article/a-christian-revival-is-under-way-in-britain/.

Brown, Colin, ed. "Church, Synagogue." *The New International Dictionary of New Testament Theology,* vol. 1. Grand Rapids, MI: Zondervan, 1986.

Bruno, Chris, and Matt Dirks. *Churches Partnering Together: Biblical Strategies for Fellowship, Evangelism, and Compassion.* Wheaton, IL: Crossway Books, 2014.

Burge, Ryan, and Walter Kim. "The Rise and Fall of Institutions." *The NAE Podcast.* October 15, 2023. www.nae.org/burgepodcast/.

Calvin, John. *The Institutes of the Christian Religion,* book 4, chapter 1. Grand Rapids, MI: Eerdmans Printing Company, Reprinted November 1983.

Cause IQ. "Christian Nonprofit Organizations." www.causeiq.com/directory/christian-organizations-list/.

Chan, Francis. *Forgotten God: Reversing Our Tragic Neglect of the Holy Spirit.* Colorado Springs, CO: David C. Cook, 2009.

Chapman, Milo L. "The Church in the Gospels." *The Church: An Inquiry into Ecclesiology from a Biblical Theological Perspective,* ed. Melvin E. Dieter and Daniel N. Berg. Anderson, IN: Warner Press, 1984.

Chaves, Mark and Sharon L. Miller, eds. *Financing American Religion.* Walnut Creek, CA: AltaMira Press, 1999.

Childress, Rasheeda, and Emily Haynes. "Drop in Giving From 2021 to '22 Was Among the Steepest Ever, 'Giving USA' Found." *The Chronicle of Philanthropy.* June 22, 2023. www.philanthropy.com/article/drop-in-giving -from-2021-to-22-was-among-the-steepest-ever-giving-usa-found.

"Church." (Compassion's Ministry Philosophy Series.) Colorado Springs, CO: Compassion International, 2011.

Clowney, Edmund P. *The Church: Contours of Christian Theology.* Downers Grove, IL: InterVarsity Press, 1995.

Colson, Charles and Richard John Neuhaus: *Evangelicals and Catholics Together: Toward a Common Mission.* Dallas, TX: Word Publishing, 1995.

Coenen, Lothar. "Church." In *The New International Dictionary of New Testament Theology.* Vol. 1, edited by Colin Brown. Grand Rapids, MI: Zondervan, 1975.

"Collect for the Mission of the Church." Book of Common Prayer Online. www .bcponline.org/Collects/variousc.html.

"Cooperating in World Evangelization: A Handbook on Church-Para-Church Relationships." Lausanne Occasional Paper 24 (1983).

Coren, Michael. "Christians Can't Blame Anyone Else for the Decline in Belief." *The New Statesman.* November 30, 2022. www.newstatesman.com /thestaggers/2022/11/decline-christianity-ons-census-uk-resolve.

Cosper, Mike. "Boomers, the Big Sort, and Really, Really Big Churches." Produced by Mike Cosper. *The Rise and Fall of Mars Hill,* June 28, 2021. Podcast, 58:11. www.christianitytoday.com/ct/podcasts/rise-and-fall-of-mars-hill /mars-hill-podcast-boomers-big-sort-hybels-warren-driscoll.html.

Cwiekowski, Frederick J. *The Beginnings of the Church.* Mahwah, NJ: Paulist Press, 1988.

David, Jim, and Michael Graham. *The Great Dechurching.* Grand Rapids, MI: Zondervan, 2023.

Deanesly, Margaret. *History of the Medieval Church 590-1500.* London: Taylor & Francis e-Library, 2005.

Deffinbaugh, Bob. "When Division Becomes Multiplication (Acts 15:3-16:10)." Bible.org. August 13, 2004. https://bible.org/seriespage/24-when-division -becomes-multiplication-acts-153-1610.

Dever, Mark. *The Church: The Gospel Made Visible.* Nashville, TN: B&H Academic, 2012.

DeYmaz, Mark. *Disruption: Repurposing the Church to Redeem the Community.* Nashville, TN: Thomas Nelson, 2017.

DeYmaz, Mark, with Harry Li. *The Coming Revolution in Church Economics: Why Tithes and Offerings Are No Longer Enough, and What You Can Do About It.* Grand Rapids, MI: Baker Books, 2019.

Collins, Glenn. "What Does APEST Look Like in Community?" (Does the Church Have a Future and a Hope?, part 4), FŌS Church. June 13, 2022. https://fos.church/conversation-notes/ydkmn-sexmc-4cz2h-gc2tp -e9cmz-f7s2k-m85s7-wdk4s.

Douglas, J. D., ed. *The New International Dictionary of the Christian Church.* Grand Rapids, MI: Zondervan, 1988.

Dulles, Avery. *Models of the Church.* New York: Image Books, 2002.

Dye, Clayton. "The College Missionary's Place in a Formal Ecclesiology." D.Min. thesis, Denver Seminary, 2023.

Earls, Aaron. "Southern Baptists Grow in Attendance and Baptisms, Decline in Membership." *Baptist Press.* May 9, 2023. www.baptistpress.com/resource -library/news/southern-baptists-grow-in-attendance-and-baptisms-decline -in-membership/.

Erickson, Millard J. *Christian Theology.* 3rd ed. Grand Rapids, MI: Baker Academic, 2013.

Eriksen, Thomas H. *What is Anthropology?* Edited by Thomas H. Eriksen and Jon P. Mitchell. London, England: Pluto Press, 2004.

EveryCampus. https://everycampus.com.

"'Every Campus' Movement Aims to Reach Hundreds of Unreached Colleges for Jesus." CBN News. July 28, 2023. www.youtube.com/watch?v=lV54js -Ykf4.

Ferguson, Everett. *The Church of Christ: A Biblical Ecclesiology for Today.* Grand Rapids, MI: Eerdmans, 1997.

Fitch, David E. *The Great Giveaway: Reclaiming the Mission of the Church from Big Business, Parachurch Organizations, Psychotherapy, Consumer Capitalism, and Other Modern Maladies.* Grand Rapids, MI: Baker Books, 2005.

Fitch, David. "Tim Keller's 'Gospel Ecosystem': 3 Dangers in a Noble Idea." Missio Alliance, September 27, 2011. www.missioalliance.org/tim-kellers -gospel-ecosystem-3-dangers-in-a-noble-idea/.

Ford, Lance, Rob Wegner, and Alan Hirsch. *The Starfish and the Spirit: Unleashing the Leadership Potential of Churches and Organizations.* Grand Rapids, MI: Zondervan, 2021.

Foxe, John. *Foxe's Book of Martyrs.* Public domain, first printed 1563.

Frost, Michael. *Mission Is the Shape of Water: Learning from the Past to Inform Our Role in the World Today.* Cody, WY: 100 Movements Publishing, 2023.

Giles, Kevin. *What on Earth Is the Church? An Exploration in New Testament Theology.* Downers Grove, IL: InterVarsity Press, 1995.

Greer, Peter, and Chris Horst. *Rooting for Rivals: How Collaboration and Generosity Increase the Impact of Leaders, Charities, and Churches.* Bloomington, MN: Bethany House, 2018.

Gregory, Brad S. *The Unintended Reformation: How a Religious Revolution Secularized Society.* Cambridge, MA: The Belknap Press of Harvard University Press, 2012.

Guder, Darrell L., ed. *Missional Church: A Vision for the Sending of the Church in North America.* Grand Rapids, MI: Eerdmans Publishing, 1998.

Guder, Darrell. "Young Life Links Up with Seminaries." *Young Life Outlook* 5, no. 1 (January 1981).

Haddad, Jordan. "Doing Ministry for the Sake of the Apostolate." *Homiletic and Pastoral Review,* January 14, 2021.

Halter, Hugh, and Matt Smay. *AND: The Gathered and Scattered Church.* Grand Rapids, MI: Zondervan, 2010.

Harper, Brad, and Louis Metzger. *Exploring Ecclesiology: An Evangelical and Ecumenical Introduction.* Grand Rapids, MI: Brazos Press, 2009.

Harris, Scott, and Amy L. Sherman. "The End and Future of the Church/'Para-Church' Relationship: A Call for Generous Partnership." Mission Increase, ND.

Haskins, Charles Homer. *The Rise of Universities.* Ithaca, NY: Cornell University Press, 1970.

Hirsch, Alan. *The Forgotten Ways: Reactivating Apostolic Movements.* 2nd ed. Grand Rapids, MI: Brazos Press, 2016.

Hirsch, Alan, and Tim Catchim. *The Permanent Revolution: Apostolic Imagination and Practice for the 21st Century.* San Francisco, CA: Jossey-Bass, 2012.

Hoge, Dean R., Benton Johnson, and Donald A. Luidens. "Types of Denominational Switching Among Protestant Young Adults." *Journal for the Scientific Study of Religion* 34, no. 2 (June 1995).

Ishee, Terry, and Angie Ward. "Loaded Terms." *The Big C Church Podcast.* August 22, 2023. https://angiewardphd.com/loaded-terms-with-terry-ishee-the-big-c-church-podcast-ep-1/.

Jones, Jeffrey M. "U.S. Church Membership Falls Below Majority for First Time." *Gallup.* March 29, 2021. https://news.gallup.com/poll/341963/church-membership-falls-below-majority-first-time.aspx.

Kärkkäinen, Velli-Matti. *An Introduction to Ecclesiology: Ecumenical, Global, and Interreligious Perspectives.* 2nd ed. Downers Grove, IL: IVP Academic, 2021.

Keller, Tim. *Center Church: Doing Balanced, Gospel-Centered Ministry in Your City.* Grand Rapids, MI: Zondervan, 2012.

Keyton, Joann. *Communication and Organizational Culture: A Key to Understanding Work Experiences.* Thousand Oaks, CA: Sage Publications, 2005.

Kim, Eugene. Guest Lecture in Reclaiming Ecclesiology. Denver Seminary. January 10, 2024.

Kim, Eugene, and Angie Ward. "What is the Church? Part 5." *The Big C Church Podcast.* November 20, 2023. https://angiewardphd.com/what-is-the-church -part-5-with-eugene-kim-the-big-c-church-podcast-ep-14/.

Klink, Edward W., III. *The Local Church: What It Is and Why It Matters for Every Christian.* Wheaton, IL: Crossway, 2021.

Koller, Tim, and Angie Ward. "A Failure of Leadership." *The Big C Church Podcast.* August 29, 2023. https://angiewardphd.com/a-failure-of-leadership-with -tim-koller-the-big-c-church-podcast-ep-2/.

Larkin, Jr., William J. *Acts.* The IVP New Testament Commentary Series, ed. Grant Osborne. Downers Grove, IL: InterVarsity Press, 1995.

Lawrence, C. H. *Medieval Monasticism: Forms of Religious Life in Western Europe in the Middle Ages.* 3rd ed. Essex, UK: Pearson Education Ltd., 2001.

Lilly Family School of Philanthropy. "Giving USA: Total U.S. Charitable Giving Declined in 2022 to $499.33 Billion Following Two Years of Record Generosity." IUPUI News. June 20, 2023. https://philanthropy.iupui.edu/news -events/news/_news/2023/giving-usa-total-us-charitable-giving-declined -in-2022-to-49933-billion-following-two-years-of-record-generosity.html.

Lopus, Al. "157 Organizations Honored as 2020's Certified Best Christian Workplaces.'" https://workplaces.org/articles/bcwi-announcements/157 -organizations-honored-as-2020s-certified-best-christian-workplaces.

Louw, Johannes P. and Eugene A. Nida, eds. *Greek-English Lexicon of the New Testament Based on Semantic Domains,* vol. 1. 2nd ed. New York: United Bible Societies, 1989.

Luasanne Movement, "The Lausanne Covenant." https://lausanne.org/statement /lausanne-covenant.

Lynch, Mikey. *The Vine Movement: Supporting Gospel Growth Beyond Your Church.* Sydney, Australia: Matthias Media, 2023.

Marshall, I. Howard. *The Acts of the Apostles.* The Tyndale New Testament Commentaries. Grand Rapids, MI: Eerdmans, 1980.

Marshall, I. Howard, A. R. Millard, J. I. Packer, and D. J. Wiseman, eds. *New Bible Dictionary.* 3rd ed. Downers Grove, IL: InterVarsity Press, 1996.

Mathison, Keith. "Historical and Theological Foundations." August 25, 2014. www.ligonier.org/learn/articles/historical-and-theological-foundations.

Matt. "The State of Church Membership: Trends and Statistics [2024]." *Churchtrac.* www.churchtrac.com/articles/the-state-of-church-membership.

Matz, Daniel X. "Generational Change in Giving and Philanthropy." *Candid.* November 8, 2023. https://blog.candid.org/post/next-generation-donors -future-philanthropy/.

McGowan, Andrew B. *Ancient Christian Worship: Early Church Practices in Social, Historical, and Theological Perspective.* Grand Rapids, MI: Baker Academic, 2014.

McKnight, Scot. *The Blue Parakeet: Rethinking How You Read the Bible.* 2nd ed. Grand Rapids, MI: Zondervan, 2018.

McNeal, Reggie. *The Present Future: Six Tough Questions for the Church.* San Francisco, CA: Jossey-Bass, 2004.

"Megachurch Definition." Hartford Institute for Religion Research. http://hirr .hartsem.edu/megachurch/definition.html.

Mental Health America. "The State of Mental Health in America." MHA National. https://mhanational.org/issues/state-mental-health-america.

Metcalf, Sam. *Beyond the Local Church: How Apostolic Movements Can Change the World.* Downers Grove, IL: InterVarsity Press, 2016.

Miller, Timothy S. "Basil's House of Healing." *Christian History,* no. 101: 12-14.

"Missions Stats: The Current State of the World." The Traveling Team. www .thetravelingteam.org/stats.

Missio Nexus webinar—Sherman/Harris—Church/Parachurch. https:// missionexus.org/events/virtual-events/#!event/2022/3/23/the-end-and -future-of-the-church-8221-para-church-8221-relationship.

Moltmann, Jürgen. *The Church in the Power of the Spirit.* New York: Harper and Row, 1977.

National Institutes of Health. "Mental Health During the COVID-19 Pandemic." NIH COVID-19 Research. September 28, 2023. https://covid19.nih .gov/covid-19-topics/mental-health.

Newbigin, Lesslie. *Sign of the Kingdom.* Grand Rapids, MI: Eerdmans, 1981.

"New Testament Exegesis Bibliography—2022." *The Denver Journal,* vol. 25 (January 2022). https://denverseminary.edu/the-denver-journal-article /new-testament-exegesis-bibliography-2022/.

Neuman, Scott. "The Faithful See Both Crisis and Opportunity as Churches Close Across the Country." *NPR.* May 17, 2023. www.npr.org /2023/05/17/1175452002/church-closings-religious-affiliation.

Niebuhr, H. Richard. *The Kingdom of God in America.* Middletown, CT: Wesleyan University Press, 1988. First published 1937.

O'Neal, Sam. "Exploring the New Testament City of Antioch." July 9, 2018. LearnReligions.com. www.learnreligions.com/exploring-the-new-testament -city-of-antioch-363347.

Osborne, Grant R. *The Hermeneutical Spiral: A Comprehensive Introduction to Biblical Interpretation, Revised and Expanded.* Downers Grove, IL: IVP Academic, 2006.

Peer, Andrea. "Global Poverty: Facts, FAQs, and How to Help." *World Vision.* April 4, 2023. www.worldvision.org/sponsorship-news-stories/global -poverty-facts.

Pellowe, John. *The Church at Work: A Manual for Excellent Church-Agency Relations.* Winnipeg, MB, CA: Hignell Book Printing, 2012.

Pettegree, Andrew. *Brand Luther: How an Unheralded Monk Turned His Small Town into a Center of Publishing, Made Himself the Most Famous Man in Europe—and Started the Protestant Reformation.* New York: Penguin Books, 2015.

Phang, Kevin et al. *The Next Normal: The Future of Christian Ministries and Churches in Canada*. Waybase 2022 National Survey Summary Report.

Philanthropy Roundtable. "Who Gives Most to Charity?" www.philanthropy roundtable.org/almanac/who-gives-most-to-charity.

Phillips, Sue. "The Spiritual Infrastructure of the Future." *Glean Network*. June 26, 2024. www.gleannetwork.org/post/the-spiritual-infrastructure-of-the-future.

Pope Paul VI. *Apostolicam Actuositatem*. November 18, 1965. Vatican City.

Post, Kathryn. "Who Are the 'Nones'? New Pew Study Debunks Myths About America's Nonreligious." *Religion News*. January 24, 2024. https://religion news.com/2024/01/24/who-are-the-nones-new-pew-study-debunks-myths -about-americas-nonreligious/.

"Putting the Parachurch in Its Place." *Jesus Movement Blog*. January 10, 2022. https://disciplemaking.church/blog/f/putting-the-parachurch-in-its -place?fbclid=IwAR1rXIQizfokssubnHYUzTh-kge_uOhhbagPfrE8G54BXg9 RVdJoDLpings.

Radmacher, Earl D. *The Nature of the Church*. Nicholasville, KY: Schmul Publishing Co., 1996.

Rainer, Sam. "Churches Are Receiving Less of Total Charitable Giving." *Outreach Magazine*. March 6, 2023. https://outreachmagazine.com/features/74316 -churches-are-receiving-less-of-total-charitable-giving.html.

Roach, David. "Church Attendance Dropped Among Young People, Singles, Liberals." *Christianity Today*. January 9, 2023. www.christianitytoday.com /news/2023/january/pandemic-church-attendance-drop-aei-survey-young -people-eva.html.

Roach, David. "Southern Baptists Lost Nearly Half a Million Members Last Year." *Christianity Today*. May 12, 2023. www.christianitytoday.com/news/2023 /may/southern-baptist-membership-drop-baptism-rebound-sbc.html.

Robbins, Stephen P. *Organization Theory: The Structure and Design of Organizations*. Englewood Cliffs, NJ: Prentice-Hall, 1983.

Rollinson, Shirley. "A Brief History of Denominations." April 23, 2019. www .drshirley.org/hist/hist21-denominations.html.

Ryken, Leland, James C. Wilhoit, and Tremper Longman III, gen. eds. *Dictionary of Biblical Imagery*. Downers Grove, IL: InterVarsity Press, 1998.

Saunders, Jon. "The Place and Purpose of Parachurch Ministries." The Gospel Coalition. August 31, 2015. www.thegospelcoalition.org/article/parachurch -ministry/.

Scheitle, Christopher P. *Beyond the Congregation: The World of Christian Nonprofits*. Oxford, UK: Oxford University Press, 2010.

Scherer, Ross P. *American Denominational Organization: A Sociological View*. Pasadena, CA: William Carey Library, 1980.

Sellers, Ron. "Generosity Is Not Driven by Income." *Christianity Today*. April 19, 2023. www.christianitytoday.com/better-samaritan/2023/april/generosity -is-not-driven-by-income.html.

Shellnutt, Kate. "Above Reproach? Fewer Americans See Pastors as Ethical." *Christianity Today*. January 25, 2024. www.christianitytoday.com/news /2024/january/pastor-trust-credibility-reputation-gallup-poll-clergy-ethi .html.

Sherman, Amy L., and Jacob Baldwin. "Churches Don't Have to Be Lousy Stewards. Here's Proof." *Common Good*, no. 11 (May 1, 2023). https:// commongoodmag.com/churches-dont-have-to-be-lousy-stewards-heres -proof/.

Schmutz, Philip. *Para-Church Organizations: A Blessing and a Curse for the Local Church*. Maitland, FL: Xulon Press, 2018.

Shawn, Haydn. *Generational IQ: Christianity Isn't Dying, Millennials Aren't the Problem, And the Future Is Bright*. Carol Stream, IL: Tyndale House Publishers, 2015.

Shelley, B. L. "Parachurch Groups (Voluntary Societies)." In Reid, Daniel G., Coordinating Ed. *Dictionary of Christianity in America*. Downers Grove, IL: InterVarsity Press, 1990, 863-65.

Shelley, Bruce, with Marshall Shelley. *Church History in Plain Language*. 5th ed. Grand Rapids, MI: Zondervan Academic, 2021.

Sheppard, Jim. "Surprise: Millennials and Gen Z are Poised to Become the Church's Best Givers." https://careynieuwhof.com/what-baby-boomers -can-learn-from-millennials-and-gen-z-about-church-giving/.

Sherman, Amy L., and Jacob Baldwin. "Churches Don't Have to Be Lousy Stewards. Here's Proof." *Common Good*, May 1, 2023. https://common goodmag.com/churches-dont-have-to-be-lousy-stewards-heres-proof/.

Sider, Ronald J., John M. Perkins, Wayne L. Gordon, and F. Albert Tizon. *Linking Arms, Linking Lives: How Urban-Suburban Partnerships Can Transform Communities*. Grand Rapids, MI: Baker Books, 2008.

Silliman, Daniel. "For Sale: Christian Ministry Headquarters." *Christianity Today*. June 2, 2024. www.christianitytoday.com/news/2024/june/remote -work-evangelical-office-headquarters-for-sale.html.

Slick, Matt. "What is the Filoque Clause Controversy? Is it Biblical?" Carm. December 9, 2013. https://carm.org/about-doctrine/what-is-the-filioque -clause-controversy-is-it-biblical/.

Smietena, Bob. *Reorganized Religion: The Reshaping of the American Church and Why It Matters*. New York: Worthy, 2023.

Smith, Gregory A., Patricia Tevington, Justin Nortey, Michael Rotolo, Asta Kallo, and Becka A. Alper. "Religious 'Nones' in America: Who They Are and What They Believe." Pew Research Center. January 24, 2024. www .pewresearch.org/religion/2024/01/24/religious-nones-in-america-who -they-are-and-what-they-believe/.

Smith, Leo Rowland. *Missional Emergence: How* Missio Dei *and Its Intersection with Transformative Learning Theory Can Move Christ-Followers Toward a Missional Lifestyle*. Ph.D. diss., Fuller Theological Seminary, 2023.

Snyder, Howard A. *The Community of the King.* Downers Grove, IL: InterVarsity Press, 1977.

Sproul, R.C. *What Is the Church?* Sanford, FL: Reformation Trust Publishing, 2013.

Staff Reporter. "A Quarter of UK Charities are 'Faith-based.'" *Church Times.* April 29, 2016. www.churchtimes.co.uk/articles/2016/29-april/news/uk/a-quarter-of-uk-charities-are-faith-based.

Stephens, Mitchell. "History of Television." Grolier Encyclopedia. https://stephens.hosting.nyu.edu/History%20of%20Television%20page.html.

Stiles, J. Mack. "Nine Marks of a Healthy Parachurch Ministry." March 1, 2011. www.9marks.org/article/journalnine-marks-healthy-parachurch-ministry.

Stott, John. "The Lausanne Covenant: An Exposition and Commentary." Lausanne Occasional Paper 3 (1974).

Tafilowski, Ryan, and Angie Ward. "What is the Church? Part 1." *The Big C Church Podcast.* October 24, 2023. https://angiewardphd.com/what-is-the-church-part-1-with-ryan-tafilowski-the-big-c-church-podcast-ep-10/.

Tanner, Norman. *A New Short History of the Catholic Church.* New York: Bloomsbury Continuum, 2011.

The Cape Town Commitment: A Confession of Faith and a Call to Action. Peabody, MA: The Lausanne Movement, 2011.

The Redemptive Nonprofit: A Playbook for Leaders. New York: Praxis, 2019.

The Traveling Team. "Missions Stats: The Current State of the World." www.thetravelingteam.org/stats.

Thumma, Scott. "Exploring the Megachurch Phenomena: Their Characteristics and Cultural Context." Hartford Institute for Religion Research. 1996. http://hirr.hartsem.edu/bookshelf/thumma_article2.html.

Thumma, Scott. "The Kingdom, The Power & The Glory: Megachurches in Modern American Society." Ph.D. diss., Emory University, 1996.

Thumma, Scott. "What Makes God Free Is Free Indeed: Nondenominational Identity and Its Networks of Support." Hartford Institute for Religion Research, 1999. www.hartfordinstitute.org/bookshelf/thumma_article5.html.

Tickle, Phyllis. *The Great Emergence: How Christianity Is Changing and Why.* Grand Rapids, MI: Baker Books, 2012.

Tillapaugh, Frank. *Unleashing the Church: Getting People Out of the Fortress and into Ministry.* Ventura, CA: Regal Books, 1985.

Tombs, Robert. *The English and Their History.* New York: Vintage Books, 2014.

UNHCR. "Refugee Data Finder." United Nations. October 24, 2023. www.unhcr.org/refugee-statistics/.

Underground Network. "How It Works." www.undergroundnetwork.org/how-it-works-index.

van der Ven, Johannes A. *Ecclesiology in Context*. Grand Rapids, MI: Eerdmans Publishing Co., 1996.

Visé, Daniel de. "Churchgoing and Belief in God Stand at Historic Lows, Despite a Megachurch Surge." *The Hill*. December 21, 2022. https://thehill.com /changing-america/enrichment/arts-culture/3782032-churchgoing-and -belief-in-god-stand-at-historic-lows-despite-a-megachurch-surge/?fbc lid=IwAR32nKRhCYfLblWAWBZDqgK8GJYbKKIXogvTbsCLuNn9zE 7JQoXJIDeBlXM.

Warren, Rick. *The Purpose Driven Church: Growth Without Compromising Your Message and Mission*. Grand Rapids, MI: Zondervan, 1995.

"What Is a Nonprofit?" National Council of Nonprofits. www.councilofnon profits.org/what-nonprofit.

"What Is Loaded Language? And Why You Should Care." USA Translate. Last updated September 28, 2022. www.usatranslate.com/what-is-loaded -language.

White, Jerry: *The Church & The Parachurch: An Uneasy Marriage*. Portland, OR: Multnomah, 1983.

White, Jerry. "Current Realities." Talk presented at Church-Parachurch Summit. Denver, CO. October 31, 2022.

"Why America Gives 2022." www.classy.org/why-america-gives/.

Wilcox, Jayne, and Angie Ward. "What Is the Church? Part 3." *The Big C Church Podcast*. November 7, 2023. https://angiewardphd.com/what-is-the-church -part-3-with-jayne-wilcox-the-big-c-church-podcast-ep-12/.

Wilken, Robert Louis. *The First Thousand Years: A Global History of Christianity*. New Haven, CT: Yale University Press, 2012.

Willmer, Wesley K., J. David Schmidt, and Martyn Smith. *The Prospering Parachurch: Enlarging the Boundaries of God's Kingdom*. San Francisco: Jossey-Bass, 1998.

Winter, Ralph. "The Two Structures of God's Redemptive Mission." *Missiology: An International Review* 2, no. 1 (January 1974): 121-39.

Wittberg, Patricia. *The Rise and Decline of Catholic Religious Orders: A Social Movement Perspective*. Albany, NY: State University of New York Press, 1994.

Wuthnow, Robert. *The Restructuring of American Religion: Society and Faith Since World War II*. Princeton, NJ: Princeton University Press, 1988.

Youngren, J. Alan. "Parachurch Proliferation: The Frontier Spirit Caught in Traffic." *Christianity Today*. November 6, 1981. www.christianitytoday.com /ct/1981/november-6/parachurch-proliferation-frontier-spirit-caught-in -traffic.html.

Yount, Steve. "Bible Reading Drops to Unprecedented Low in America." *Denison Forum*. August 15, 2023. www.denisonforum.org/biblical-living /bible-reading-unprecedented-low-america/.

Zarnecki, George. *The Monastic Achievement*. London: Thames and Hudson Ltd., 1972.

Missio Alliance

Rooted in the core convictions of evangelical orthodoxy, the ministry of Missio Alliance is animated by a strong and distinctive theological identity that emphasizes comprehensive mutuality, hopeful witness, and the church in mission. Missio Alliance addresses the most vital theological and cultural issues facing the North American church in God's mission today. In partnership with InterVarsity Press, Missio Alliance offers a line of books authored by a diverse range of theological practitioners. These resources are selected based on how they address and embody these values and the unique contribution they offer in equipping Christian leaders for fuller and more faithful participation in God's mission.

Remissioning Church
978-1-5140-1055-6

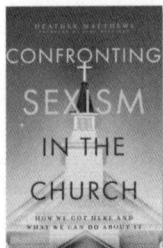

Confronting Sexism in the Church
978-1-5140-0818-8

Faithful Politics
978-1-5140-0749-5

Plundered
978-1-5140-0774-7

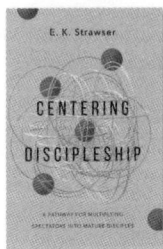

Centering Discipleship
978-1-5140-0706-8

Finding Freedom in Constraint
978-1-5140-0431-9

missioalliance.org | ✕ f ⃝ | missioalliance